Team Up For Excellence

Dedicated to my wife, Carol, and sons, Mark and Paul,
for their understanding of our own teamwork and their love.

Team Up For Excellence

Allen Mackay

Illustrated by Brian Withers

Auckland
OXFORD UNIVERSITY PRESS
Melbourne   Oxford   New York

Oxford University Press, Walton Street, Oxford OX2 6DP
Oxford   New York   Toronto
Delhi   Bombay   Calcutta   Madras   Karachi
Kuala Lumpur   Singapore   Hong Kong   Tokyo
Nairobi   Dar es Salaam   Cape Town
Melbourne   Auckland   Madrid
and associated companies in
Berlin   Ibadan

Oxford is a trade mark of Oxford University Press

ISBN   0   19   558268   3

Cover designed by Nikolas Andrew
Set in Times by Egan-Reid Ltd
Printed in Hong Kong
Published by Oxford University Press
1A Matai Road, Greenlane
PO Box 11-149, Auckland, New Zealand

Contents

Foreword

The industrial production system in the West is founded on the views of Frederick Lewis Taylor, who believed that:

> The employee is (1) a constant in the production system, (2) an inert adjunct of the machinery, prone to inefficiency and waste unless properly programmed, (3) by nature lazy, (4) his main concern is self-interest. He must therefore be tightly controlled and externally motivated in order to overcome his natural desire to avoid work unless the material gains available to him are worth his effort. (Knowles and Saxberg, 1971)

This conviction was still in vogue in the 1970s and it took an American, W. Edwards Deming, working with the Japanese, to make Western industrialists realize that there were better ways in which to view employees. However, the real tragedy is that many organizations still see their people this way and utilize them accordingly.

The focus for change was the demand for improved quality of product and gains in business efficiency. But there was no way that management could succeed on their own and they slowly came to the realization that Taylor was totally wrong.

Having people understand customers' requirements, be in control of their tasks and work together in teams to continually improve the way they carry out their work has proved to be the most effective way to manage an organization.

However, people, on their own, cannot bring about the change required without leadership and vision from management. Setting the environment and developing the direction with the people are essential ingredients of success. Also, there is the need to establish a methodology that people can follow. Merely putting a group of people together to work on issues that concern them cannot in itself produce any lasting benefit as they are unlikely to work on activities that are important to the business. Hence, it is crucial to have a methodology that adopts a systematic approach to improvement and which ensures that the team works on issues which will benefit the business as well as themselves.

The approach outlined in this book is derived from the experience of the author in changing parts of organizations from the Taylor model to a Total Quality Management, teamwork-driven environment, supported by management, involving everyone and, most importantly, making use of the skills and intellect of everyone in the group. People can develop their technical and personal skills at their own pace, comfortable with the fact that they will be rewarded for this knowledge and skill. This book describes a systematic approach to team building, organizational development and business improvement through the personal development of the people doing the work.

So, team up for excellence!

Wayne Squires
General Manager
National Technology and Management Services
    and Total Quality Management Institute of New Zealand

Introduction

The success of effective teams has been clearly demonstrated throughout the centuries in the sports arena. With sport, nationality and most other factors have not been a barrier to achieving success. Effectiveness has been the result of individual efforts, combined and focused, with a common passion and desire for achieving an agreed objective or result.

This success in sport can be replicated in business if the company's members operate as a team, and if their directed role is the achieving of agreed targets.

The creation of teams can work in many areas of a company's operation, even if at first glance there seems to be no real need for them or no value to be gained from their creation. Time after time it has been proved that they do work, and that they work in a variety of companies and environments.

Teams are not just small groups of people within a company's departments, nor are they restricted to the company's staff. They also include company-wide inter-departmental members, as well as suppliers, subcontractors and others who contribute in some way to the final product or service delivered to the paying customer.

Companies that have formed and operate effective teams have variously:[1]

- changed the way the business is run
- increased customer satisfaction and retention
- achieved a reduction of over 35 per cent in operating costs
- achieved an ongoing reduction in all costs
- increased productivity over 30 per cent in twelve months
- improved revenues
- increased margins and yields

---

1. Team accomplishments are recorded from: Saudi Arabian Airlines (Engineering Department); Air New Zealand (Logistics Department); Toyota, New Zealand.

- made the company a fun place to work
- gained the trust of staff
- achieved empowerment of staff
- achieved alignment of staffing and workloads.

I have had first-hand experience of the many positive changes wrought by companies that have instituted teams. I have worked for some of these companies, acted as a consultant to others, and had discussions with the staff of many of them.

If you are comfortable with the way most businesses are run today, please be aware this book is not about maintaining the status quo. Rather, it takes a hard, sometimes brutal look at the common or 'normal' organizational structures, business practices and people systems found in most companies and analyses the reasons for their ineffectiveness.

Many business philosophies and practices, such as Total Quality Management (TQM), Just In Time (JIT), and Theory Of Constraints (TOC), achieve a negative reputation within companies as being 'flavour of the month'. This is quite often because they are just that. Even with the best of intentions, management lacks the ability to follow through on the implementation of the selected strategy because of obstruction caused by the company's existing policies, procedures and organizational structures. These existing structures and systems can also make it difficult to implement those things that are just 'good common sense'.[2]

How can we say we understand business, when businesses are in the poor state they are today and economies reflect the health of those businesses? Businesses and economies have been struggling because management and non-management people believe that company structures are fairly rigid and that the market-place is only slightly less so. They have relied on or expected the government and banks to protect these rigid structures.

---

2. 'Why TQM Fails', *IS*. (1992) April.

When tariffs are reduced or removed, or the value of currencies is floated (usually the wrong way), labour strikes for what is felt to be entitlements and the market (the customers) goes to the competition. The shout is, 'Unfair!' Rather than companies changing to be flexible to customers' wants and needs, the cry goes out for more protection and help from the government. Companies seem to be asking: 'Why should our structure and working methods change? Don't the customers understand our problems?' The thinking appears to be that the inability of companies to change and be responsive to the customer is normal; therefore, the customer should understand and put up with it. This acceptance of an inability to change is a major flaw in most organizations. Another serious fault is not knowing how to respond to customers' needs and wants.

In most companies the staff have usually inherited their organizational structure and its characteristics. To question it would be a sacrilege and could mean certain death to a career. It takes a brave person, someone with tremendous faith in his or her beliefs, to stand up and question the status quo.

Defence of the status quo is often phrased thus: 'We have always done it this way in the past and the company was successful in the past, and may be today, so why should we change anything?' However, believing that the success of the past breeds success in the future has led to the demise of many product lines, services, and companies.

What does it take to create a company environment and structure that will allow an organization to be responsive to the market and which, at the same time, will guarantee that the organization makes a profit and sees its profit grow? It requires consistently excellent performance in ensuring that the customer is attracted by and satisfied with the company's products and services. It is this satisfying and memorable experience that establishes the long-term customer base which is essential as a foundation on which to build a strong company.

To achieve this performance, we need to create a company environment that:

- is trusting, rewarding, and enjoyable
- enables the right things to be done right, first time
- enables staff to be sensitive and responsive to the customer
- enables the implementation of constant improvements to business practices
- creates empowered and enabled staff at all levels
- develops good internal and external communications
- has salary rewards not tied to job titles or promotion
- allows technical and personal skills to be rewarded
- supports teams of staff working towards corporate goals
- recognizes individual as well as team effort and results
- achieves the best possible return on investment
- promotes job security from company strength
- makes all of the above *habitual* behaviours.

A daunting goal? Not really, if it is approached through a simple, speedy system in which people and machines do only those things that add value to the final product or service which the customer is willing to buy, and where they eliminate or minimize those things that do not add value.

Many companies have hopped onto the 'team' bandwagon; and for many this has been to their cost, because the team system has failed, through the lack of a structured and planned effort, to ensure its long-term success. The major problem lies in a lack of understanding by staff of what their company as a business is trying to achieve, and of how they and these new teams will help achieve it.

Successful implementation firstly requires all company members to understand the company's mission statements, goals, and business plans. It also requires these same staff to accept wholeheartedly the tough decisions that need to be made.

The company needs to develop a system in which the role of emotions is kept to a minimum and decisions are based instead on an abundance of quality information. Likewise, the system of the 'dictatorial directive' needs to be changed. Merely moving away from the environment where things must be done or not done simply because an individual or minority group demands it would be a major success for most companies.

It is all too easy for everyone to get onto a bandwagon that is popular with the executives of the company. When the team hype rages through all staff levels and business activities, it is very easy to forget that the real goal of the company is to make money, always through its satisfied and excited customers. How many of us were either part of a company or worked in conjunction with a company when the 'computer craze' hit businesses in the 1970s? The feeling that computers should be bought raged through companies, regardless of whether they required them or not. It was very easy to get approval from company executives to buy computers, even though the evidence of real requirement was vague or, in many cases, tissue thin. I spent time in companies which felt they desperately needed computers and so purchased them, only to discover that, two or three years later, they were still trying to find needs or uses for their electronic boxes of tricks. And, as most in business are aware, many companies did not buy only one computer, as bigger discounts could be had if ten or thirty or a hundred units were purchased.

What was the real problem in these cases? Although some companies made a success of the computer, in many cases success was very limited. Computers had been presented to the business world as the only way to get a major competitive advantage in the market-place. So companies set off on a purchasing spree, without determining a true need or seeing a business advantage whereby the computer could add value to the customer service, product, or bottom line.

Information should have been sought with regard to what the company's customers would get out of the computer purchase. If no advantages to the customer were seen, then justification for a purchase should have been very difficult.

Another problem with new ideas is the feeling that: 'A new idea works for a similar company, so it must work for us too.'

But do we know why it worked for the other company? Maybe the idea worked only because other changes, not visible to us, were made at the same time. Do we really understand the impact the idea will have on our business? Have we thought it through? Have all staff concerned been involved in and trained for the proposed change in the work environment, and have they consented to it? Most importantly, do we know whether it will contribute more to tomorrow's bottom line and/or increase customer retention?

Teams are an extremely valuable tool for a company if they are constructed to operate effectively and are motivated and given clear objectives. 'Effectively' and 'efficiently' are very overworked words. What do they really mean in the context of the company?

- Effectively: *doing the right things*

This means ensuring that we know what the customer wants and ensuring that the company strives to meet those requirements. 'Knowing what the customer wants' can also include anticipating or conditioning customers' desires and expectations.

- Efficiently: *doing the right things right, first time*

This means ensuring that the functions and tasks which make up processes are carried out correctly at the very first attempt, to avoid any re-work or the passing on of any incorrect information.

In this book we look at a radical way of doing business and a powerful tool for team building, growth, development, and continual improvement. What follows is not a discussion of theory but rather a set of practical and proven steps which have provided, and in many cases exceeded, the successes listed as examples earlier.

It is no surprise to the staff of companies who have tried and failed that building long-lasting teams requires an effective system and inspired leadership. Much of this leadership cannot be delegated and those who have delegated too much have felt the pain and wrath of being involved in the resultant fiasco and failure.

We must ask ourselves: what have the past few years of business decisions shown us?

A brief list could include the following.

UK:
- 5600 homes per month being repossessed in 1991 (a 53 per cent increase over 1990)
- 166 companies per day going bankrupt in 1991 (up 60 per cent on 1990)
- a movement from manufacturing to services (from 60/40 per cent in 1980 to 27/75 per cent in 1991)

USA:
- both Ford and GM announce $1 billion plus losses in 1990 and greater losses in 1991
- GM announces 72,000 layoffs and 21 plant closures up to 1994–95
- Hyundai (Korea) achieved the most car sales in California

NZ:
- unemployment in 1991 at 14.8 per cent (35 per cent increase on 1990)
- building permits down 38 per cent (residential) and 74 per cent (non-residential) on 1990 (includes 10,000 office space jobs in buildings planned in 1988, now cancelled)

A sure sign of the times is a case in New Zealand in 1991, where people competed for a free car. All they had to do was keep their hand on it the longest (with breaks only to relieve themselves). The winner was a woman who managed to keep her hand on the car for 100 hours (4.17 days). And the prize? An eight-year-old Honda City!

Clearly, poor business performance and recession have not been brought about because management wanted to make poor decisions. However, old-style decision making resulted in companies being content to continue producing products and supplying services which customers were willing to pay for yesterday, but which they would not be willing to pay for today and tomorrow. The staff probably expressed their concerns and desire to change the ways of doing business. Management, on the other hand, were taught that only they knew best and that non-management staff should 'leave their ideas and opinions at the door'.

Companies have relied heavily on consultants to assist and direct them. However, consultants have often been there just to deliver the message companies wanted to hear. If they did not, then they probably would not have been employed.

So who can we blame? The answer is: no one. Management, staff and consultants were trained and educated in the methods that ensured the 'accepted ways' of doing business were put forward and implemented. Occasionally, a different way of doing business may have got through, but on the whole the system itself filtered out most of these. The system's filters were the individuals, tiers and bureaucracy of companies, local government, central government, and so on. The total business environment was one of maintaining the status quo, and it was 'normal' and expected that existing or similar company structures should be preserved. Decisions were made only at the top. This applied to a high majority of businesses, and resulted in:

- management feeling reasonably secure in their positions but generally being out of touch
- staff at most levels feeling they had almost no way of improving the business or their work area, and reflecting that feeling in their work
- customers responding negatively to the environment of the company and expressing this by taking their business elsewhere
- margins, profits and market share being reduced
- continual staff layoffs and cost-cutting.

A customer cannot be counted as retained if you keep only 20 per cent of his or her original business. When customers become short-term 'visitors' or defect from the company, it indicates clearly that profits will soon diminish.

Summary

It is vital to recognize that the team and the individual are both extremely important. What is needed is an understanding of how to structure, develop and reward both teams and individuals without detriment to either, while at the same time shedding costs, improving margins, and being extremely customer-responsive.

We must not apportion blame. Instead, the purpose of this book will be to consider and promote some new options that will deliver excellent results today, tomorrow, and in the future.

The successes of teams have been demonstrated by companies like Toyota, Nissan, Harley Davidson, British Airways and Federal Express. The problem for companies has been how to shift to an effective team system that will create a permanent and empowering change throughout the company and that will be responsive enough to constantly make the quality improvements needed to achieve customer satisfaction and excitement.

In the following chapters, we shall look at the practical implementation of such a system.

1

The past and the need for change

It may be hard to see the need for an environment different from that existing in any specific company today. This is especially true if the company is making a profit. However, looking at a list of companies similar to your own that have disappeared, for whatever reason, in your area, country, or around the world, will help bring home the cold reality of the need to change in these tough economic times.

The good old days

Since the industrial revolution it has been mainly the rich who have managed businesses. 'Managed' is not entirely correct, however, as it was not necessary for the rich to be able to manage. After all, they had the money and owned the factory, plant, plantation, workers' homes, the company store, and so on. New generations of managers were usually the sons or daughters of these rich owners. They knew of no other way to manage or, indeed, of any need to change. If someone set up their own new business, the chances of it being any different from all the rest were small, though there were exceptions.

Understanding people and their needs was not generally considered important, but longer hours, faster work rates and quotas were. The boss/owner was always right and 'just get it done' was the answer to many problems hindering production or service delivery.

So what is different now?

What is different now, and why the need for change? Doesn't company success in the past guarantee success in the future?

The answer is a resounding 'No!' It takes vision and a strong will to see beyond what is currently acceptable and profitable.

Successes of the past guarantee absolutely nothing in the future. Take for example the Swiss, who in 1968 had 60 per cent of the world market and an estimated 80 per cent of the world profits in watches. The decisions of the past should have taken them into a solid future. But obviously they did not. The Japanese now dominate the world market with the quartz crystal watch, which the Swiss themselves invented. The Swiss thought the lack of a main spring and gears meant that the quartz crystal watch would never catch on, so they didn't even protect the idea. In 1968 at the annual Watch Show, Texas Instruments and Seiko saw the invention, and the rest is history.

The Swiss still make excellent watches, though for a much smaller market, and their mistake cost them over 50,000 jobs.[1]

The reason for change is simple: customers' demands change and are always changing. It is as simple and as complex as that. Understanding customers' wants and needs is more vital today than ever before. Customer needs and wants are never a clearly defined set of standards. Instead, their wants are a varying set of peculiar perceptions changing with their moods and the environment in which they find themselves. What was acceptable to the customer yesterday may not be acceptable today. This is the nature of the market and the world that businesses currently find themselves in.

Sensitivity to customers

Let's take a simple look at advertising. Advertising is mainly used to achieve market gains by alerting customers to the advantages, pleasures or fulfilment to be gained from using the product or service offered. But isn't most advertising really a crutch? Isn't advertising used because the company does not believe the product or service it is offering is good, exciting or memorable enough in itself to bring the customers back willingly? What would happen if the company stopped all advertising? There are companies that do not advertise but which have extremely good profit and growth figures year after year. Some of these companies have grown to $US6 billion in fifteen years or have achieved 'zero defects' in deliveries to the Japanese market-place.[2]

The company's fear of ceasing advertising arises from its lack of contact with or sensitivity to the customers. Many companies

---

1. Joel Barker, *The Business of Paradigms*.
2. Remarkably successful companies who do not advertise: (1) The Limited retail stores, USA, (2) Golden Needle Company, California, USA, (3) Interlock Industries, New Zealand (who have achieved 'Zero Defects' according to President Mr S. Young).

feel they have to advertise because the customer base is too broad, varied, remote, and so on. This excuse is then accepted and used to hide behind.

Some companies have now started 'SWAT teams' whose task is to keep in touch with customers who have not used the company's products or services in an acceptable time span. These companies have realized the need to stay in contact with as large a customer base as can profitably be maintained.

Chain stores issue plastic cards to customers who provide only their names, addresses, and phone numbers. Customers are given a five per cent discount whenever the card is used, and the SWAT team is fed computer information on customers who have not used the stores for a set period. The same customers are called and invited back to the store, or are sent publicity material and vouchers to entice them back.

Some insurance companies pay their salespeople a premium for every year a customer stays with the company, so customers in turn are kept informed of good news and encouraged to stay.[3] These premiums can increase after the five- or ten-year period is reached. Customer retention requires that salespeople and the company listen to customers and be continually sensitive to their needs and wants.

A lack of customer sensitivity is the death knell for any business. Companies must strive to understand what motivates the customer, though this is not always an easy task, as the following story illustrates:

> Thomas Edison worked for years and years in his bedroom to perfect the lightbulb, and late one night after these many failures he finally succeeded. He was very excited and he turned to his wife and exclaimed, 'I did it. I did it! I have finally succeeded!' And his wife said, 'That's great honey, now can you turn off that light and come to bed!'

To remain sensitive and responsive to customer needs and to

---

3. Great-West Life Assurance, Englewood, Colorado, USA pay salespeople more if customer retention targets are achieved.

keep costs right (not just down) are the goals of today and the future. The competition no longer comes only from local firms, for many companies do not just sell to local communities. Even the local dairy or bakery may sell beyond its local population.

Today globalization is at a level where businesses and countries influence others through loans, investments, political pressure, membership of key organisations (EEC, OPEC), and so on. As an example, in one year Japan spent some $US400 million trying to influence American legislation for the benefit of its own industries.[4]

The need for a global company effort

Some disadvantages of current company structures and ways of doing business are:

4. P. Choate, *Harvard Business Review.* (1990) Sept/Oct.

- lack of sensitivity or responsiveness to customers
- lack of customer satisfaction and excitement
- inability of individuals and teams to change the way companies do business
- poor levels of quality and lack of timely information
- inability to make the company more profitable today and even more so tomorrow.

At the very least, the company as a whole must ensure cost effectiveness and customer satisfaction. The new way of doing business applies not only to those companies not doing well or near bankruptcy today. It also applies to many companies which are making the same decisions today that they were making one or two years ago when they were making a profit, and which are hoping that the same decisions will make the same profit tomorrow and in the future.

How can a single person or even small group within any company be sensitive to the majority of customers? The answer is that they cannot. Such sensitivity involves the whole company working as a team—not teams of individual prima donnas or individuals who sit in a team for their own gains, but rather a global company effort that will allow the customers to have their expectations met or exceeded. And met at the instant they should be, not following a remote management conference a month later or after discussions that result in a 'nice' letter being sent too late to stop the defection of the customer to the opposition.

The biggest failing of companies is an inability to see that the decisions of yesterday are not necessarily the best that can be made, even if they brought about profits. The perceived profitability and success of today may be only a result of external factors such as the state of the economy, rather than of the state of the company itself.

Summary

The past provides many examples of how not to do business. It also offers some excellent examples of success and inspired leadership. Recognizing that the future is for change and taking along everyone in the company to effect change will achieve competitive advantages previously only dreamed about.

What would it be like if everyone in the company questioned everything they did at work every day? The driving force for this questioning would be to meet customers' expectations or exceed them if appropriate. Changes could be achieved more simply and through shorter processes, while adding to the whole company's ability to deliver quality products and services consistently and reliably, and at competitive prices and margins.

Quite an exciting time lies ahead, but it requires a commitment to change and team building and leadership very different from that of the past.

2

The beginning

The company environment

Whether a company is long established or newly formed, its performance and the way it is perceived by the customer are determined by the work environment of its staff. This environment can be happy, productive, enriching, rewarding, profitable, and growth-orientated. It can also be exactly the opposite of this.

The company environment determines staff members' perceptions of how the company 'feels', and it can include the culture, procedures, and levels of trust and honesty. The environment dictates whether company members feel they can be innovative, whether their ideas are accepted as practicable and looked at with honesty, whether open discussion is acceptable, and whether the staff members and customers are considered to be important.

The environment is a result of many factors, such as:

- the degree of trust existing among staff at all levels
- the number of staff levels within the company
- the importance of the individual's effort and results as compared with those of the team
- the amount of effective communication
- the overall system within the company.

The environment is created to ensure the company's people can respond to the customer at the right moment. The customer can be defined as: (1) the company's internal departments, shops and employees, wherever they may be, who expect services or products from your area, whether paid for or not, and (2) the external companies, agencies or individuals who buy your products or services but who are not employees of the subject company (most often defined as the paying customer).

Trust

Trust is something that has to be worked on over many years. If someone within a company says he or she will do something, then it should be done. If it isn't, then an explanation must be given, in a timely manner, to enable trust to be maintained. In many companies, trust is not a strong point, and poor

communication only helps break down this chief ingredient in good company performance.

Customers are sensitive to the posture of a company. The company can have a great advertising campaign but when customers are actually dealing with the company's staff it does not take them long to assess the company's real degree of sensitivity. If the staff, at whatever level, are frustrated, then customers will feel the results of this frustration and will probably take their business elsewhere.

Staff who ask the customer to 'Please understand, I only work here and I have asked for this or that to be changed for the last three or five years!' will chase customers away. No matter how good the advertising is, if the whole company is not working towards satisfying the customer, the money spent is wasted. Everyone must be made to feel part of the company team and each person and each idea must be considered to be important.

So, the style of management for today and the future is not dictatorial, but rather one where trust and participation ensure that all staff feel important. How important? Try to imagine your company operating without anyone there! That's how important!

Trust is something that can only be built up and contributed to through consistent demonstration by each person. Cleaning up the company's structure and methods will enable better communication and trust to be developed.

Staff levels

The number of staff levels in the company has a major impact on the overall business. Too many decisions are made with the person first wondering: 'If I do make this decision, will I still have a job three to four months from now?' Any wrong decision can be the one that ends a career, because decision making reflects the number of steps up to the top of the company's promotional staircase. This has proved itself to be true far too often in the past. So how can we obtain better and fuller information on the areas in which we must make decisions? How can we allow the people willing to take some focused risks to do so, without worrying about the effect on their career progress?

It is vital to realize that decision making is not the sole right of management. With 80 per cent of tasks being carried out at the front-line or workforce level, there should be a mountain of decisions being freely made there, in alignment with those at all levels of management. They *should be* made there, but often this is happening only in the best companies. The majority of companies do not have a structure which allows decisions to be made freely and be seen to be freely made. Every employee wants to be viewed in a good light within the company, so the need to avoid making mistakes drives staff away from making decisions at all.

Who suffers in this environment of apathy and/or self-protection? All who are part of it, but most importantly it is the customer who suffers. Will the customer stay around in this environment?

Importance of the individual versus the team

Let's take a look at a company I know very well and examine the method of rewards and development within it. What emerges is all too familiar in many companies worldwide.

The primary goal of a company should be to deliver to customers products or services that will enable the company to make money today and even more tomorrow. For this to happen, people must be motivated towards achieving that goal and be rewarded for their performance. So how does the company in question reward good or excellent performance?

Unfortunately, it uses the standard method, i.e. individual promotion and individual merit rewards. This method ensures that the individual is rewarded and it also makes clear to everyone how to do well—as an individual. It confirms the need to work as an individual, remain an individual and stay away from teams or groups. There is no incentive for individuals to help fellow employees, because someone else will only receive the promotion, reward, or credit, and to help others is to risk being associated with any complaints directed at others. To help others is to risk falling behind in the merit race.

We have here a normally structured company with a normal reward system geared to the individual. It has created an environment where the important thing is just to keep your head low and claim anything good that comes along as yours. In this environment, if an unusual job is given by the boss to an individual staff member, it is seen as a reward for a job well done or a skill possessed by the individual.

Team synergy has been documented as a component in the major successes of many companies and is vital to long-term success.[1] The importance of individuals and teams must be kept in balance. How this can be done is discussed in later chapters.

---

1. Team synergy documented by: Toyota (worldwide); Fisher & Paykel, Auckland, New Zealand; Karelle Personnel and Training, Auckland, New Zealand; and the companies where the author has worked (worldwide).

Career development

The importance of the individual is also fostered by a lack of career development. It is hard for a person to know exactly what he or she should be doing or what is important when career development is unclear or not specified. In turn, individual training tends to be vague because of this uncertainty.

Training is often used as part of the reward system in companies. If performance accords with the boss's particular likes and dislikes, then training is granted. Whether the training will add value to the staff member's contribution to the department or is in line with promotional effort is usually not known, and quite often not considered important. Training is often done willy nilly, without planning or merely as the result of a personal judgement made by the boss. Sometimes the training used as a reward will be prompted by the only training leaflet to have crossed the boss's desk in the last four weeks. Often it merely allows the boss to meet his or her expected quota of training hours.

Building up specialist skills is a great way to make an individual feel important or invaluable. To return from a vacation or a couple of days off and find a big pile of notes that only you can handle is a sure sign of having achieved this goal of being indispensable. What is lost in this activity of self-importance is the number of customers who will not wait for your return and who will take their business elsewhere. There can be no multi-skilling for these staff members: the company has ensured, through its promotion and reward schemes, that the individual reigns supreme. The customer will be lucky to rate anywhere nearly as high.

Effective communication

Staff always seem to complain about poor communication. Ninety per cent of companies I surveyed had a majority of staff complain about poor communication. Companies where decision making takes excessively long periods of time are companies with big problems, because the time it takes for the information or decision to get to where it is needed is usually too long for it to have any real relevance. The result is that companies can be on the down escalator and only the customer and front-line staff are aware of it.

One of the benefits of effective teamwork is good communication. Teams need:

- immediate decisions
- access to quality information at the right time

- access to decision makers or, better still, a decision maker on the team
- a decision-making process with the minimum number of steps.

Limitations in communication are usually due to the view that information is power—usually power for an individual, and power to be used against others. Keeping information to yourself makes you feel important. This is a common way of ensuring that rewards and promotions are limited to those with the information. If customers suffer and the cause cannot be traced back to you, then that is seen as an acceptable reason for a lack of concern about not passing on information. The information holder is also most likely to be the one with a good 'promotional glow' when the time comes to apportion blame.

The system within the company

The system within the company can best be described as the methodology of doing business. This applies to any kind of business and includes all manual, mechanical, and electronic methods.

The Policies and Procedures Manual

The system is critical to the business. This can be illustrated by asking this question: When I get up to go to work, do I say to myself, 'I must get to work to read the Policies and Procedures Manual'? In my own research, not one single staff member in numerous companies answered yes. Yet many companies have such a manual and it is seen as the law by which the company operates.

So, what is this vital document used for in most companies? It is used to apportion blame. It gets a very high usage when something goes wrong. Staff will go through it with a fine-tooth comb to see who have stuck their necks out too far, and there is immense relief among those who find that their own necks are not at risk. For those not immediately inside the blame/shame arena, getting trampled in the 'disassociation' stampede is the only fear.

This system is very common but is disliked by almost all who work within it. The system has endured primarily because it is felt that it is too hard to change it.

If it takes an amendment to the Manual (which can take months) for changes to be made within the company, little is achieved other than the stifling of innovation and improvement. If the Manual adds nothing to the final product or service delivered to the paying customer and does not add to the company's ability to be customer-sensitive in a timely manner, why have it?

The Policies and Procedures Manual is just one example of how companies have become stuck. The past has demanded the need for such books and there are even more books published to tell you how to write policies and procedures you probably would never otherwise have dreamed up. The creation of these and many other documents is due to the historical lack of trust among members of staff in so many companies. These documents are supposed to be an accurate and an up-to-date series of standards and limits. When people attempt to work to the rules laid down in them, it usually becomes clear just how inaccurate, out of date and unhelpful the documents are.

Monthly reports

In another part of the system, we demand that all sections, departments and divisions send in monthly reports which are supposed to measure performance against certain standards. Reports can often be a poor method of ascertaining what is really happening or of getting the whole picture. Asking for a monthly report is like asking your children to write down what kind of month they had at school, expecting them to relate all the events in a few pages, and also expecting to gain a real

understanding of what has been going on at the school. These expectations are seldom met.

In a bad month the report is very thick and is written by the area's in-house lawyer, or seems to be. Conversely, if the month has gone well, the report is thin, but equally meaningless.

When I join a new division or company I get on the mailing list for as many monthly reports as I can, in order to get an early, but poor, indication of the whole company. It is a *poor* indication, because as anyone who fills out a monthly report knows, it is often at best a CYA (Cover-Your-Arse) document.

On one general manager's desk, I saw more than thirty monthly reports of eight pages each, received from departments and stations worldwide during the first four days of the month. Each page was filled with 'data', but there was no way that this could all be called useful 'information'. A further study of the general manager's own time showed he had only 15 per cent of his time available to devote to these reports and the departments and stations over which he had responsibility. The rest of his time was used on promotion committees, merit committees, official tours, and so on.

It was impossible for anyone with his workload to read and understand this number of reports, but the reports kept coming month after month and year after year. Therefore, all the hours spent at each section, department and station to produce the reports were next to useless.

Much of the data was also useless. When I questioned some of the data contained in the reports I found major reporting errors. One figure reported was 'productive manhours'. I wrote to eleven departments asking them to send me their definition of this term and the mathematical equation used in arriving at the figure. I wasn't surprised to receive eleven totally different definitions and equations. So all the data that decisions were based on in the past did not even compare apples with apples. It was a simple but major problem of a system which demanded reporting for the sake of reporting.

What would happen if the monthly reports suddenly stopped? Would it really make a big difference to the system of doing work? I would say that in many companies it would not. In this case the monthly report was simply a security blanket.

To those producing them, there are two very distinct sides to monthly reports. First, there is the burden of producing them. Secondly, they can be a very useful tool for keeping the corporate bosses away and letting those who are reporting get on with the job at hand. In neither case are they the tools of effective communication they were originally designed to be. What if the monthly report was stopped? This would mean those receiving the report would have to get out and about to see the business first hand, and this is certainly not what management today has been groomed for in the vast majority of companies. The companies themselves are not structured so as to have systems in place to allow management to see what is going on in the different work areas.

The way you do business

It would be possible to go through many of the components of 'the system within the company' but that is not the point of this book. The point to note is that the business must be structured to ensure that the company's staff have the energy, willingness and ability to direct their best efforts towards satisfying all the customers which the company can profitably maintain. The best way to achieve this is to change the way of doing business so that all individuals feel important and are rewarded. Contributions to team efforts and results must also be rewarded, and the customer must be recognized as part of the team.

Understanding the business

Let me ask you to consider a question. Think of other companies in the *same* business as yours. Take a minute to think of three things that makes your company really different from others, from a cost point of view. If you are doing the same business, what makes one of you more profitable?

Just list three things that make your company unique. Your sixty seconds start now.

1. _____
2. _____
3. _____

Please try to complete this before going on.

If you found that hard, then you are like most people I have asked to do the exercise.[2]

---

2. From 286 people surveyed only three could state unique differences when comparing their company with similar companies. These 286 people were from six companies in four industries.

Let's look at an example. Take shoe manufacturing companies in the USA. All these shoe manufacturers buy materials, pay labour rates, train their staff, need machinery, face location problems, subsidise medical expenses, support marketing fees and so on, but their costs are different. Why is this? The main difference is *the way they do business*. This applies to all like companies I have compared or worked with or for. Even information from journals and authoritative magazines shows this simple fact to be true.

The way they do business involves waste rates, junk piles, stacks of inventory or work in progress, late collections of payments due, and so on. Rarely is it the amount of automation or the numbers of computers used. If you listed location, remoteness, exchange rates, small population, and other similar factors, I would suggest that with a bit of research you could find a company with similar problems, limitations, or concerns.

So the answer is, simply, the way we do business. When going to work I have to go through thirteen traffic lights. Every day I hit at least three of these on red. Only on one day have I hit all the lights green (or yellowish) and I talk about that particular trip often. I was able to have two cups of coffee and to get through a stack of work before the time I would normally have arrived at work. Is that not what companies are trying to achieve: all green lights for the customers and business? The situation they are trying to achieve is one where everything possible (that is profitable) is done to please and excite the customer, and where risks are acceptable when, though perhaps not profitable in isolation, they repay themselves by winning long-term customer loyalty.

Company levels

If your company has fifteen levels of job titles, then it has fifteen layers. There are all sorts of arguments about how many layers there are, but the fact is there are fifteen. It can be said that there should only be two: management and non-management;

but to state the matter in these terms would be an over-simplification. Or would it?

If the company has fifteen layers, and so carries out down-sizing, re-alignment, flattening or 'slash and burn' techniques but does not change the way work is carried out, the results will be failure in most cases, as illustrated in Figure 2.1 (Method 2).

What work is carried out and the way work is carried out determine the costs and the customers' perception of its value to the price. Costs are a direct result of work. If the company restructures and allows the old work and work habits to remain, then failure will surely follow—and what will the company do next year? Why, restructure again. It would be better to stay with the status quo (Figure 2.1, Method 1) than adopt Method 2.

Figure 2.1 Results related to method adopted

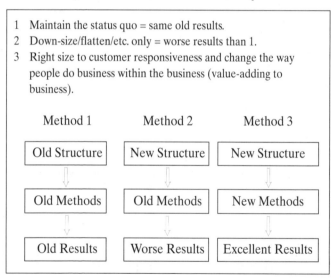

1   Maintain the status quo = same old results.
2   Down-size/flatten/etc. only = worse results than 1.
3   Right size to customer responsiveness and change the way people do business within the business (value-adding to business).

If your company has eleven inspectors on a line to get a job done and my company has one inspector to do the same job, I should be able to do the job more cheaply (at one eleventh of the inspection cost, all other things being equal). The difference is not location or automation; I simply rely on the workers to do the job right and don't try to 'inspect-in' quality.

What will happen if companies remain as they are today? What if we perpetuate an environment in which only the individual is important, where career paths are vague, and where individuals know only in the short term (if at all) what is expected of them? What if location, automation, foreign exchange and so on are the great excuses to be continually hidden behind?

These companies will not have an environment where staff can meet or exceed customer expectations. Nor will they have an environment of trust and individual and team development to make them places of focused risk taking. In the future, customers will no longer be fooled by advertising, gifts and prizes or excuses which result in short-term business or second and third chances.

It is time for companies to structure themselves to enable all people in the company to deliver the right products and services at the right time to meet or surpass customers' expectations. To achieve this the people in the company must carry out work according to methods that add value to the company's products and services and that enable them to constantly improve all areas of the business they are involved in (as illustrated in Figure 2.1, Method 3).

The path to the correct company environment is a system of focusing on people, the customer, and the company. The system does not rely on one person, department or idea but is a system which makes the process habitual within the company. It is this ability to be permanently absorbed into the fabric of everything everyone does that makes it so effective. And this ability to 'team up for excellence' can be, and should be, an enjoyable experience.

Summary

The need for the company environment to be right is

paramount. After all, it is people who make the product or provide the service to the customer. A machine will not ask after your family, your arthritis, your promotion, or how the kids are doing at school. The environment in which people work and interface with customers is critical. The best company structure, the neatest forms and the best machines cannot match the tenacity of motivated company employees in delivering the right products and services at the right time and at the right level of quality.

The remarks made so far are simply to show that the way a company does business is the vital factor in success, and that there must be a better way. This better way will be discussed not as theory but as real steps which need to be worked through. The very real problems encountered, from previous experience of implementing of the system, will be discussed along with the solutions used to overcome them.

We can summarize our goal as the creation of a company and environment which:

- is *trusting, rewarding, and enjoyable*
- enables the right things to be done right, first time
- enables staff to be sensitive and responsive to customers
- enables the implementation of constant improvements to business practices
- creates empowered staff at all levels
- develops good internal and external communication
- recognizes individual as well as team effort and results
- achieves the best possible return on investment
- does not use promotion as the main method of salary reward
- rewards technical and personal skills
- supports teams of staff working towards corporate goals
- makes all of the above habitual behaviour.

The steps needed to organize for a better business are not easy or gentle. The system takes strong will and determination, but once in place such a system can overcome the limitations of many of today's companies.

3

Why teams?

'Why have teams? Are they really any better than hard-working individuals?' 'We tried teams before and they did not work very well, if at all.' 'We have teams and we still rely heavily on individuals and quite often the teams thing gets in the way and slows everything down.'

How familiar these comments are. And most of the time they come from company members who want teams to work. However, in many cases, the team concept was applied to existing company structures and business methods and was therefore doomed to failure.

Communication

I have found that one of the main advantages to be gained from a team approach is the creation of an environment which promotes effective communication. The effect of applying teamwork to the processes and operations throughout departments, areas and the company as a whole is remarkable. The ability of each team member to contribute to the end result and to *know how he or she contributed* makes the work more rewarding and the workplace more congenial.

Knowing what is happening, and why, takes much of the mystery out of the decision-making process and helps staff grow through learning by experience.

Some staff fear that teams will take away their ability to be free thinkers or fringe thinkers. They voice concern that the need to conform to the team will blunt their ability to think 'outside the square'. Fortunately, the result of teamwork is exactly the opposite. With a greater understanding of the business and its problems and successes, plus a fuller understanding of the customers' needs, such fringe thinkers can enjoy almost limitless scope for innovation. They may not see this at first, and it can take six to nine months before they do see it.

Management's role is to coach and counsel these and other staff through this period of adjustment.

Culture

Many companies support an environment and culture which prevent their being successful. The basic flaw in these culture is the *lack* of a team effort and the compartmentalization and territoriality that ensue. In one company I know, the work areas were so strongly compartmentalized that, not only was it physically impossible for one employee to answer another's telephone in the same office, but it was accepted as normal that no one would even want to do so.

In another company the walls were there to stay but did not go quite to the ceiling. Rather than go around the wall to ask a question one staff member used to write his question on a slip of paper attached to a clip. The paper and clip were thrown over the wall on the end of a piece of string and the sender would wait for a tug on the string to indicate that the answer was ready. I was there for half a hour during which time not a word was spoken between the two participants.

Many, many times I have found phones ringing in an office where some of the staff present were not busy. When they were asked why they did not answer the phones, the various answers included: It was not their phone; they were on their break time; the office closes at 4.30 so whoever it was will have to try again tomorrow.

These attitudes and activities are large neon signs indicating that profit slumps are occurring today and will continue into the future if not corrected. Sales and marketing can be doing really well in the field or market-place but this attitude back in the office, plant or assembly-line area will not help close sales or generate repeat customers.

Clearly, the company requires a *total team effort.*

What is a team?

A team is two or more people working together to achieve common goals. These people may or may not be in the same office (intra- or inter-departmental), may or may not be on the same shifts, may or may not be in the same location (within the city or country), and the duration of working together may be short-term or long-term. Team members may or may not be from the same company.

Thus there are two types of company team: intra-departmental and inter-departmental. The improvements that these teams work to achieve are often the result of suggestions, sensible or radical ideas, or stray comments.

Not all improvements to the business will be perfect. Perfection is not the only goal of any idea or improvement pursued, for each idea or improvement (even if flawed) brings the whole *process* of doing work closer to perfection.

The process of satisfying or exciting the customer should be targeted towards perfection. Perfection, however, will always be elusive, because customers are continually changing their wants and desires. Nevertheless, it should be sought in order to challenge the team continually and constantly improve the business.

Intra-departmental teams

Many will, I am sure, find that the profile of a normal company department set out below reflects the current state of their workplace. These features can be found from the shop floor to the top of the company. It is easy to see the problem this group will have in satisfying the customers' needs in a timely manner.

The following example is based on a company I know. A typical department within it features:

- four very separate work areas
- full and half walls throughout
- the ethos of 'my phone, my desk, my job' reigning supreme
- multiple job titles (up to eleven)
- 'specialists' everywhere
- three unions
- average length of service in the department: 18.5 years
- promotion from job title to job title
- importance given to individuals
- annual merit bonuses normal for all individuals
- no meaningful measurements of internal or external customers' service or satisfaction levels
- limited knowledge of how the company is doing.

The need for an effective and efficient intra-departmental team is thus obvious.

The company's total team will, in almost all cases, be made up of smaller teams that are intra-departmentally created and which work towards common goals. Whether this means a section of an assembly line or a shop or department will depend on the size and organizational structure of the company.

Inter-departmental teams

Members of these teams must be able to make clear decisions based on the facts before them, for the good of the whole company team. This means a major shift in the way these team members do business. The background of these members has usually been the 'who is right?' and 'blame/shame' arena. But inter-departmental teams do not exist to argue the rights or wrongs of decisions made by various individuals; rather, they must ensure that the best business advantage is gained from the decisions made. The best business advantage is gained only when everyone attending these meetings presents the best quality of information to everyone. Everyone must give up ownership of empires, territory, functions, assets, and so on. Unless this ownership can be given up, the best business advantage will not be gained.

Proof of the need

As we examine and review tasks performed by team members in the following chapters, we can use a 'proof of the need' yardstick.[1] This will help us decide whether the task in question is really necessary. If we cannot 'prove the need', then the item will be put in a *waste* list. Waste can be defined as anything which does not add value to the end product or service delivered to the paying customer.

We cannot just drop those task items that fail the 'proof of the need' test, as there may be some area within or outside the company where the result of the task many be needed. The task may be wasteful to us but necessary to another part of the 'company' team, which includes suppliers and others. We must, if possible, assist that other area in finding an alternative source of the product or service.

Staff involvement

We have now decided to enter the exciting and challenging business environment where the 'company team result' becomes the main focus of all efforts. The company team result will be a measure of various agreed indicators, and one that is extremely important is the measure of staff involvement.

Staff involvement is a direct result of training, education, trust and total empowerment to get on with improving all

1. 'Proof of the Need' is a phrase coined by Dr Juran of Juran Institute Inc., USA. Dr Juran is recognized as one of the foremost leaders of the 'Quality Revolution' worldwide.

aspects of the task of cost-effectively meeting and exceeding customers' expectations. This can be achieved only by training staff to new levels and then getting out of their way.

Summary

Most current business environments ensure that the majority of people who work there become focused inwards on their own personal needs, survival, empires, and job tasks. There is no clear, common urge driving them to satisfy the customer, because that task is perceived as something that has to be done during the day and is quite often something that just 'gets in the way'.

Company members cannot achieve the best business advantage if they are protecting their 'territory', and territory always seems to cover all things—except the customer.

Our 'proof of the need' yardstick will help us decide whether or not to eliminate the need to do the task under review, and will help us balance the effect of the decision on our own and others' areas.

Why have teams? Staff who are capably led and who are involved, motivated, trained and empowered will bring about remarkable improvements and changes in the way business is done. When the focus is steered away from individual territories, the result is the customer and company team—one of the most refreshing environments in which to work.

4

How to get started

Examining the way business is done by departments

To start, take a look at the way business is done today by your departments. This does not involve an immediate restructuring of your company, rather you should simply ask yourself: Are the tasks that are being done today in these departments the *right* tasks, and are they being performed *right*, the *first time* and every time they are carried out?

It is vital that an examination of the way business is done by departments uses a Do-It-Yourself approach wherever possible. Facilitators can be used to help the department's team leaders in their examination and to ensure that the objectives of the examination are adhered to.

An examination can be done in one department or within a whole company without initially disturbing the existing structures. However, the examination will soon prompt a desire for change, and for the implementation of better ways of doing business. Many of the company's staff members will be astounded by how easy the process is.

Remember that everyone is now heading down a path on which everything is going to be challenged. This sounds fine until one or two or five of *your* areas are challenged. Like all good people, we find it easy to inspect everyone else's back garden but want others to keep out of ours.

Forming the first team

It is useful to bring together the management from different role areas within one department so that they can discuss their known and new-found problems within that department. It is much easier to solve problems this way. Also, it is a good idea to start with supervisors and middle management. They are among the hardest groups to change in any company, for they have the most to lose as they give up many of their accepted roles as decision makers to become leaders and cheerleaders instead.

Let's follow an 'example team' through the process of restructuring the company by way of a system that produces startling, excellent, and permanent results.

First in our example, the department created a team of management staff to look at its structure and business practices. This team was made up of those five to eight management staff with expertise in the department's various role areas.

Bringing these management staff together as a team allowed

those unfamiliar with other areas within the department to question many things other members considered normal. Many of the functions and tasks questioned, challenged and changed were thought to have been set in granite by those who had worked there for many years.

Although the departmental manager was part of the team, he was instructed to be present at the meetings for brief periods only. Keeping the manager's attendance at meetings to a minimum at this stage has proved successful, for this is a stage of adjustment of attitudes for many, and if the boss is present many management staff can be too conscious of 'company politics' putting forward ideas. It also allows the departmental manager to keep in touch without dominating or unduly steering the meetings.

The facilitator helps the leader, through discussions prior to the meetings, and by offering the occasional word of advice and direction when required. A good facilitator will say almost nothing while a meeting is actually in progress.

The first team formed was drawn exclusively from management, as it would have been wrong to have involved staff who could possibly have been phased out in the resultant department restructuring. In reviewing the management structure the same would generally apply, with the senior management reviewing the levels of management immediately below them.

As stated earlier, looking at the way business is done will naturally change the way the company is structured. In one area of a department the team worked through the tasks and decided to shed 80 per cent of what was being done at that time. There is no way the existing number of staff could stay in that area after a change of that magnitude. Staff were not all made redundant or dismissed, but the changes did call for some major rethinking and re-alignment.

The purpose of the review of 'the way we do business' was to enable the company to discard many of the problems and bureaucracies and much of the waste brought about by management decisions of the past. Those decisions may have had the approval of small numbers of managers, but this new economic age demands that the company is structured to improve constantly through the use of *all* its people.

We did not move from the old way of doing business to the new one because we wanted to cut costs or down-size or pursue any of the common goals that can tear a company apart. The purpose was *to improve the way we were doing business and to improve the overall business results.*

Form a quality structure

A group of company staff were trained as facilitators and trainers prior to the start of restructuring. Their roles were to:

- train all company staff in Quality Management
- facilitate inter- and intra-departmental teams
- assist, advise and instruct management on how to adopt and operate the new philosophy
- ensure the use across the company of common business language, techniques, business tools, reporting, etc.
- be the communications hub and point of request for assistance in the quality and business change process.

The facilitators all came under the control of one senior manager or director, which made them totally independent of any department within the company (see Figure 4.1). This is vital, for if everything in the company is going to be questioned, there has to be some steering and guidance. Common methods, business tools, presentation formats and so on also have to be followed and used. The same applies to the training of company staff in the use of these applications.

Figure 4.1 Quality structure

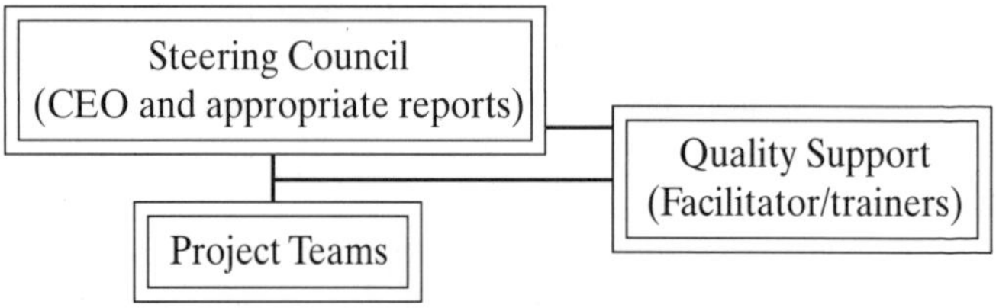

Steering Council
(CEO and appropriate reports)

Quality Support
(Facilitator/trainers)

Project Teams

Measure where you are today

The following is a step-by-step application which has proved successful in both small and large companies. We shall take one department as an example, but note that other departments will be doing the same things at different speeds and with varying results throughout the company, depending on how they are currently structured and how they carry out processes, functions, and tasks.

It is important first to measure what you are doing before you start down the path of overall team building. These measurements might include budgets and actuals for operating costs, staff numbers, overheads, assets owned, office sizes, and a host of others. It is also important to find out the equations used to obtain numerical and other results, as these will most probably change when progress is made. Having both the measurements and equations, or at least some of them, will allow improvements to be measured and judged. They allow people to prove to themselves and others that this process really works, and they make it easier to show the scale and nature of the results. They also provide a focus for celebrating the gains made along the way, which is important for all effective teams and leaders.

We (our team of eight, and one facilitator) had now:
1. formed a management team of 'challengers'
2. compiled a list of measurements

Determine what you are doing

The next role for the team in the example department was to determine what we were actually doing at that time.

Our team worked eight hours per day for five days a week on this task because everyone became very involved and enthusiastic; this has proved to be the case with most teams— twelve-hour days and six-day weeks are common. Rarely is there a request for extra payment because team membership, enjoyment of each other's successes and the ability to really change the way the company does business become addictive for all participants.

The list of what we were doing was made in a brain-storming

session. The brain-storming consisted of everyone shouting out what the department was doing in each team member's area of expertise. This generated quite long lists from all the department's areas tabulating all the tasks we were performing at that time. It was, and always is, frightening to hear just how authoritatively members of the team shout out what their area is doing today. At no time did they feel there could be any other way of doing business and they considered everything being done in their area to be vital and indispensable.

It is at times like this that leaders can appreciate what the staff throughout the company must have gone through in the past to achieve even limited changes to their environment. It is wrong to blame the staff; they have been groomed by the company's structures, policies, environment, and previous leaders.

We had now:
3. determined what we were doing

Determine what you should be doing

The next team task was to determine what the department should be doing:

- *not* the location of the department
- *not* its size, number of phones, desks, tools, etc.
- *not* who should be in the department
- *not* how many staff should be there
- *not* the skills needed
- *not* the budget required.

This task is extremely hard for most groups or teams who attempt this stage. It requires a strong facilitator and leader to keep the task's aim clearly in front of everyone, especially when your own 'sacred cow' becomes dinner for all. It is difficult discussing your sacred cows without prejudice, especially if you only recently got your sacred cow in place or have the reputation of being the resident expert. To have to explain to others a unique task or function, which only you have knowledge of, means giving up what is perceived to be a 'personal' advantage over everyone else. Some people will never be able to do this and will elect to leave the team, department or, in some cases, the company. Some will give partial information in the hope that this 'flavour of the month' will pass and the old ways of doing business will return. However, once the path detailed in this book is entered upon, there is no going back.

To achieve this step of defining what the department should be doing requires four things (see Figure 4.3):

- Company Mission Statement
- Company Business Plan
- Department Mission Statement
- Department Business Plan.

Businesses cannot have effectively operating departments, areas, divisions and regions if they do not know, with extreme clarity, the direction the company is taking.

In our example company, and in many other cases, not all of the above were available. However, we did have the company mission statement and department mission statement.

It is worth noting that for the department to accomplish its mission and fulfil its business plans it was necessary to get the confirmed support of other departments and areas. Too often departments write missions and objectives without getting the support of other departments at the concept stage (see Figure 4.2) and most of the missions and goals prove impossible. Remember to get everyone's support for the objective early, so that as the year progresses each department knows the goals of the others and knows what to expect by way of support from the other parties.

Figure 4.2 Jointly agreed objectives

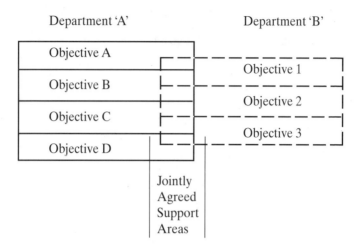

At this stage, patience is required. The team will work to find the missing pieces needed to put together the company strategic plan, company mission statement, and company business plan.

Once our team had done that, we determined the mission and business plan for the department. This process alone makes clear what everyone in the department, area or company is trying to accomplish.

Putting mission statements and business plans up on the wall, in the hope that someone will read and understand them, is usually ineffective. Mission statements and business plans should be discussed with all staff regularly so that everyone has the opportunity to understand and maybe even improve on them. For many of the team this was the first time anyone had ever sat down with them and really allowed free discussion.

Once everyone had agreed on the mission statements and business plans, and understood them, the next step was possible: defining the functions and tasks our department's staff members must perform to enable us to achieve our mission.

These are the next and final levels in determining what the department should be doing (see Figure 4.3).

Figure 4.3 What should be carried out that adds value

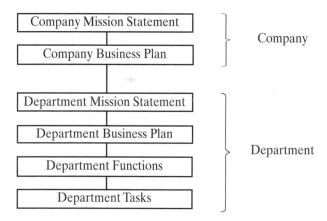

The clarity this brings to the study is invaluable. Without this stage, it is impossible to see how the real value-adding functions and tasks can be determined; the omission of this stage was always a problem with past methods.

The mission statements and business plans were then put into packs and given to each team member for review and discussion. This discussion proved most helpful. It took three to four days to cover the main areas, and the following occurred in that time.

- All of the mission statements were discussed, pulled apart and rewritten to say the same things more clearly, and to reflect the team input.
- All the *general* areas of work and topics identified were discussed; absolute details are not important at this stage.

Further discussions continued long after the initial three to four days, both inside and outside of meetings. (This becomes an ongoing habit once introduced. The constant communicating and questioning will not disappear once started in effective companies and teams.)

By the end of the initial discussions everyone had a clearer picture of what the department was supposed to be doing and achieving, and this became the common goal for the whole team. If nothing else was achieved, this clarity and unity was a major gain, and the quality of the team's work and efforts improved because of it. This was only a very small step towards where we were going, and it was the first 'buying in' to the process for many of the team members. The excitement of experiencing how easy it really all was made the team members want the process to be made habitual and institutionalized within the department and company.

There were still some doubts on small points, but the big picture was now clearer to all team members. This was probably the first time we could actually be called a 'team': we now had common goals, understood the bigger picture, and had a better understanding of each other and each other's work areas. Importantly, we were losing the need to be 'I'-orientated and were now looking at supporting the concept of 'we', where each still contributed as an individual but could personally develop more and enjoy greater influence as part of the team.

Our discussions gave us consensus. That is, while not necessarily agreeing wholeheartedly with each part of the business plan and missions, we could all live with them. We were then able to start determining what functions would enable the fulfilment of the business plan.

It should be noted that, in an ideal world, the whole company would be reviewed at the same time, but this is not always an option. Not only is that task deemed too large in some companies (which is not valid if a well-planned approach is used) but also the old culture and regimes quite often need 'proof of the need' to change. The 'proof of the need' may only come from an example of success within the company. Even then it may be very difficult to change minds.

The answer is always the same in these cases. Give an example from within the company that will cause heads to turn, and get the corporate groups to start asking: What is your area doing so differently that makes the results so startlingly better?

It can be fun and exciting to be part of the team which is leading the way, and causing those heads to turn.

5

Determining functions and tasks

At this stage, it is important for everyone in the team to contribute to the end result. This helps everyone buy in to the end result, but also allows each person to contribute as an 'individual' in the old sense, before letting go of the old way of doing business as individuals. Once they have made their contributions at this point, most people will settle down to being effective team members—all they want is a chance to shine.

For this stage, the team broke up into specialist areas for two or three days to compile two lists (see Figure 5.1). These were:

1. A list of five or so *functions* which the specialist area had to perform in order to achieve the business plan.
2. The *tasks* which had to be performed to enable the functions in (1) above to be accomplished.

Specialist areas are defined as people or sections within the department that carry out functions which are unique when compared to the remainder of the department. Examples include administration or press shop, or areas where particular skills may be needed, like welding, accountancy, shorthand, chemistry, etc. This process of defining functions and tasks is not tied to any one area of a company but is universal.

Our team limited itself to the functions we could accomplish without taking anything from any other department, and the same applied to the tasks. This was because the rest of the company was doing the same and a better result would be achieved later if we each sorted out our own back gardens first. As mentioned before, the review must be done throughout the company: if the review is limited to your own department this effectively allows those in other areas of the company to remain comfortable with doing what they have always done.

The function determined was very broad: 'Ensure maintenance of effective communication through written, electronic and verbal methods'. This function encompasses tasks such as producing monthly reports, sending and receiving telexes, completing forms, handling mail, filing, attending meetings, and other related 'doing' tasks. Note that functions should begin with 'ensure' and be of a broad nature: these are *high level* functions. (See Figure 5.1. A reproducible blank form is also provided.)

Figure 5.1 Function to task logic

Function:
1.   Communication—Ensure the maintenance of effective communication through written, phone, electronic and verbal methods.

Tasks:
1.1 Provide morning briefings to senior management.
1.2 Determine area of problem and advise concerned staff of their actions.
1.3 Maintain and update appropriate databases.
1.4 Maintain adequate records of critical cases and findings.
1.5 Monitor VHF and HF radios where appropriate to give the earliest warnings to concerned areas.

The team met again and discussed openly the findings of each of the specialist groups. It was not until about this time that questioning what others said could be done openly. It takes time to develop the ability to question the performance, rather than the performer, of any skill or task. We were not at that stage yet, but were well on the way to building trust between team members.

To assist team members in questioning functions and tasks,

Function to Task Logic

Function:
No.__

Tasks:
__.1

__.2

__.3

__.4

__.5

all were trained in a method requiring application of the phrase 'proof of the need'. This method ensured that, if the function or task did not add value, then it would not be done, for it would certainly add cost.

Every function and task must have 'proof of the need' applied to it. With the company working as one team, everyone can be questioning everything, every day, with the results being the implementation of one, ten and perhaps one hundred

improvements daily. In this way, real competitive advantages are gained.

Among other results of the 'proof of the need' exercise there emerged some extremely shocked team members. Many of the tasks that had been seen as necessary in the past were clearly shown as not necessary at all. In one area the tasks were reduced by 80 per cent. Some areas dropped many tasks but picked up others which they discovered they should have been carrying out.

The benefit of doing just this one major exercise proved the credibility of the process, and the taste of success was sweet. Now the team members wanted to progress even faster. The ability to change things was on all the team members' minds and in their conversations. The fuse had been lit!

We had now:
4.   defined what functions and tasks needed to be done

6

Environment and single job titles

We now had to determine the type of environment that would give the best results for the company and department. Since the environment either enables or inhibits people, it is a key area of competitive advantage. The environment desired for the company and department should determine the structures put in place, *not* the other way round. In our case a team environment was considered to be the best.

To see how this decision was reached, we can take a look at a truly logical company growth pattern (unlike that seen today in the majority of companies).

The company in our example is newly formed and only one person, the owner, is employed. She will:

- buy the raw materials and the tools
- do the preventive maintenance
- make, market and sell the products
- deal with all customers
- work with the bank, accountant etc.
- know the state of the business, and so on.

As the business grows the owner decides she must get some help and hires two more people. Now, will she put one person in one office, the second in another office and herself in a third office with walls and every other form of communication barrier between them? Will she only talk to the other two when she chances to see them or only at the monthly meeting? Probably not! These would be the dumbest things she could do.

Using logic and common sense, she would try to have them all share the same desk if possible, talk all the time about the business's direction, plans, problems, customers' wants and desires, and so on.

It makes you wonder then, why the office in the department, which is the subject of this book, was split by walls and structured to make communication next to impossible unless a staff member walked thirty feet to a fellow staff member who was only four feet away.

When our one-person company brought in new staff, would she have given them titles such as 'Senior this' or 'Junior that' to make sure they knew their position within the company? Would she have given them titles to make sure they kept their ideas to themselves when in the presence of a 'Senior' anything?

It all sounds so ridiculous, but isn't that exactly what most companies are like all over the world?

I used to coach and manage up to seven basketball teams in a single season, and at no time did I find it helpful to team building to give out 'level' titles. It was also not fruitful to tell half the team something with the other half sitting behind a wall somewhere else. This coaching role was the first hint of management's new function in the changed environment being designed by our team.

It is worth noting that at no time did the team decide it needed superstars. Superstars do not exist everywhere and they can destroy many of the teams they join if they cannot be team members first and foremost. If they cannot, they are not required in that team.

It became clear to our review team that job titles did very little to promote the type of environment we were trying to create: a team environment. This was one of the biggest shifts in thinking among the team members up to that stage. The realization that titles no longer played a part in the new environment caused more than one member to feel like running away, and most said so.

We decided upon a team environment because the review showed that multi-skilled staff would give better value to the customer, to the company, and to themselves:

- *Better value to the customer* because, as a team member, each staff member would have to contribute to any customer enquiry and be responsible for the quality and reliability of the product or service delivered. No longer would it be OK to push just anything out to the customer. As a team member, each person would be able to contribute constantly to improving the products and services.

- *Better value to the company* because, as a team member, each staff member would be empowered, encouraged and trained to constantly improve the processes of doing work and to enlist the help of others in making these improvements. Multi-skilling means that the team members are of greater value to the company and that their decisions are based on greater knowledge of the customer, company and business. The ability to deliver quality products and services more reliably because of personal contributions to the company's processes makes the work environment more enjoyable.

- *Better value to themselves* because, as a team member, each individual would be trained and developed to be better his or her job and to contribute to the decision-making process, thus having a greater opportunity for personal growth. Team members would know what is expected of them and know how to progress within the company and be part of a structured reward system.

Thus it was decided that a single job title for all staff members was best. (This excluded the management team, which was later renamed the Support Team and also reduced to a single level.) The single job title would eliminate the feeling of one person having dominance over others merely because of job title. It would eliminate all the old jealousies and suspicions regarding another person's eligibility to hold a particular title.

The single job title raised many questions, including: Who could do what? How would the person know his or her skill levels without a graded salary system? How do staff develop from whatever point they are at on the salary system to the next or higher levels? Who would do the assessments and how often would they be done? How would the personnel section fit into the department and what would be their roles and that of the manager? These were all critical questions, and they will be answered as we progress through the following chapters.

The team's last two decisions were very difficult to make. However, to have the team members step outside the exciting atmosphere of the team meeting room into the cold light of day was another challenge altogether. This is why the process must be well planned and why all team members must tear the plan up and reconstruct it together. It is only when every team member is sold on the idea and has contributed fully that they are ready to meet the challenges that lie ahead.

We had now:
5.   determined the type and style of environment

Reaching the end of the fifth step had taken just ten days—no time at all in a company's life-span, and the gains made were greater than any others achieved in the previous fifteen years.

The five steps taken up to this point had been painful at some stages, and difficult at varying times for different team members, depending on their beliefs. What enabled these decisions to be made was the application of the 'proof of the need' yardstick at every stage and to every question. When applying the yardstick to the need for multiple job titles, a need was not proven. Questions raised during this process were as follows.

1. What about seniority?
Answer: Is seniority necessary to carry out the function or is it a hangover from the old pay structure? It added no value to the task, function or customer so a need was not proven.

2. What about status within the department?

Answer: Status was not shown to add value to the work to be carried out by the department. Job titles actually destroy teams as they mean someone is dominant over someone else. So individual status from job titles was not proved to be necessary.

3. How about promotions in the new environment of one job title?

Answer: Promotion from one job title to the next is the old company way. It usually rests heavily on length of service as do merit bonuses. We have to reward the individuals' development of skills and personal attributes, not length of service or job title. So promotion via job titles was not proved necessary.

4. What will the unions say and how do we convince them of the one job title concept?

Answer: Can the unions today deliver a system that rewards skill development? No, but this process can. Can the unions provide each staff member with a career path? No, but this process can. Can the unions empower staff members to change the way the company does business? No, but this process can. What the team concept is offering the staff is unique and so powerful that it would be impossible for unions to say no to it. After all, it's what the unions have been trying to achieve for years. (Note: 'team' here is actually the company, but in this instance it is confined to the subject department.)

5. How do we get the individuals to work together?

Answer: A presentation to all departmental staff will be made and each member will be given a handout detailing the new concept to read and discuss. The structure of rewarding and developing staff must be in line with the concept of teams and single job titles (discussed in Chapter 7). The new structure and system of doing work and salaries must be in line with teamwork and balanced against the needs of individuals.

7

The Matrix Concept and Rewards

Problems with promotion

For a long time companies have been heading for serious problems with regard to staff development and promotion. Radical change is needed, in the way we promote and pay people, to allow executives to create companies that reliably produce quality products and services, gain markets, improve margins, strengthen the company, and provide long-term employment.

It is necessary to challenge every system of reward and promotion within companies today, because almost all are perceived to be totally set and immovable. This is certainly not the case, but those who try to change these systems will usually find themselves in either the frying pan or the fire.

We can illustrate the problems and absurdities of the traditional system of promotion with the following example.

Objective: We want to promote someone to a position that he is not going to like and from which he will destroy the spirit of all those around him. We know, and so does he, that he cannot do the new job very well. Those he left behind now mistrust him. He has taken his skills away from where they achieved the best business advantage for the company, customers, and himself. He now dreads the next annual appraisal.

A horror story? Isn't this the worst possible way to treat the individual, the company and the paying customer? In the best cases, promotion results because the individual has performed well at tasks or in function or area. However, those skills which caused the individual to be promoted are usually not completely applicable to the new position.

To take another example: a skilled and experienced mechanic is promoted to the position of foreman. The first thing that happens, in most cases, is that he locks away his tool box for good, except of course, for the odd weekend job at home. Why did he get promoted? Because he is such a good *mechanic* and the company wants to reward him through his pay packet. If the company doesn't, maybe the competition will and he may leave. The only 'permanent' method available in the normal organization is to step him up to a higher job title.

But there is a flaw in this system, because he is expected to be a good *foreman*. There is the possibility that he will be, but he might not be comfortable in that role. Perhaps, even after training and discussions, he sweats every time he comes to work because he knows he cannot do the job well. If he does not like being a foreman, there is every chance he will not be good at it. Everyone around him will suffer, along with the performance of his whole area. Perhaps he likes being a foreman but is very bad at it. Again, everyone around him will suffer.

While these are real possibilities, there is another part to the picture: the reason he got promoted in the first place. He had excellent skills in his previous position, which are now effectively lost. With most of his time spent as a hands-off foreman, who is going to produce the levels of quality and productivity equal to that lost through the promotion? The staff left behind will not. They will not be pleased that they have been passed over and that 'Joe' got the promotion instead.

They also know that 'Joe' got promoted because perhaps he used some of their ideas or suggestions or was quicker off the mark in getting to the boss. This obviously does nothing to improve the environment of the work place. It simply confirms to everyone that to get the next promotion one has to climb over others, and that the old structure and old ways of gaining the boss's eye are the best. This is not restricted to a mechanic-to-foreman promotion, but is also true for every occupation and level within the company.

Why was 'Joe' offered the promotion and why did he take it? Simply because it is the intended method of permanently rewarding people within the current organizational structure. It is *intended* because the very next appraisal could mean it is not so permanent, if Joe is found to be a non-performer in his new position. The skills of a good mechanic have been wasted, because the organizational structure dictated that we must promote to reward someone to any real degree.

Of course, there are always a good number of promotions that work out very well. The staff enjoy their new jobs and they perform well at them too. The problem lies in the loss of the skills that brought recognition and the feeling among those left behind of being passed over, because there was only one position for ten staff to go after.

Also, it takes time to develop the full level of skill required in the new position, so there may always be an initial gap after a promotion occurs, unless there has been a good deal of grooming done ahead of time. Most organizations do intend this grooming to happen, but it is not always possible as they are often preoccupied with daily operational problems. There is also a reluctance to groom people because it can threaten the job security of the groomers or their own aspirations towards promotion.

What we have discussed is 'the way we do business' and the case of 'Joe' is just one example of the way most organizations work. There must be a better way!

The single job title

After some long and very questioning meetings, our team agreed that, if a new system of salary or pay could be put in place, then a single job title system was really the best one. The team felt that this system would extract from the staff and their department the best performance for the sake of the company and the customer. It was thought that a single job title would:

- do away with dominant and subservient roles
- necessitate skill development for reward
- broaden the skills of specialists and introduce multi-skilling generally
- encourage participation in all work and decision making
- generate a team structure for all members and necessitate personal team membership
- simplify and enable staff growth planning
- create value-adding training ability
- allow training targeted to individual needs
- clarify and target team training.

And, importantly, a single job title system would:

- achieve greater customer satisfaction
- produce the ability to question and improve work processes
- improve productivity, reduce costs, and improve margins
- improve the value of each staff member
- improve communication.

Leadership

All of the above benefits still require leadership that is inspired, knowledgeable, and in touch. There are numerous leaders in today's companies who would rather apportion blame than investigate problems themselves. They are often out of touch with the real changes and events over which they think they have control.

Within the review team, it was obvious that an inspired and in-touch leadership was forming. In the beginning they were not aware of it, but as time went on everyone in the team began to change until they were constantly demanding more and more changes to the company environment to give greater satisfaction to staff and customers. As well, they went from feeling entitled to their jobs and perks to feeling that they were earning their rewards.

All the team members had to experience the hard work of changing themselves before they could attempt to change others effectively. It was important that, when creating a completely new environment for their staff to work in, they should have experienced and made adjustments to that new environment themselves during the previous two to three weeks.

In the beginning, when those from outside the team raised questions and concerns, I would be the one who gave out the answers or explained how much better this new system was than the current hierarchical style. After the three weeks had passed it was the team members who were doing the explaining and, importantly, they did so believing every word. I was able to sit back and have confidence in their explanations. After all, each one of them had designed and, through consensus, arrived at the solution.

They had moved from an environment where emotional arguments, jealousies and personality conflicts were the norm to one where logic, facts and reason held sway. This made it easier for them to sell their new ideas because they could express them logically and with conviction.

It was, and always is, exhilarating to see and experience this transformation in people.

Rewards

The next very difficult decision to be made in this exercise concerned the methods of rewarding individual staff and teams, and in this the team were on very new ground.

Firstly, it is vital that rewards match the ultimate goal: to obtain from the department the quality of work that will achieve our initial objective of creating a company system that is extremely customer-sensitive and which results in customer satisfaction. The salary or pay system must reward the staff's technical and personal skills, create an environment of teamwork, effort and cross-training and must enable staff to know what is expected of them in their work and how to progress.

As the days went by, it became easier for the team members to accept the decisions they had agreed to previously. This does not happen easily. The team members would go home in the evenings and discuss some of the less sensitive items with family or friends from work. This is natural because they were now part of a team situation in which everything could be, and was, questioned. If you bought a set of quality tyres from a garage or quality clothes from a store at one-third cost, you would get excited and tell everyone who would listen. So it is with people

who get involved in an environment of trust, exploration and innovation where 'their' ideas are really considered and actioned.

The only problem was that their family and friends would give the team members all the old reasons for not changing things: that it would be just a flavour of the month affair and they would not really be able to change anything; they might alienate themselves from workmates; benefits or jobs might be lost; recognition for work done might not be forthcoming; there might not be payment for any extra work done as part of the team.

It took many meetings for the team to lose the old styles, habits, and fears. The old ways of doing things were comfortable ways, and it takes time to dispense with them completely. They may be kept on hold in case they need to be put back in place. It was easy to agree to some things in a meeting and then two days later have the old ideas and culture turn views around again.

Now that the consensus decisions on single job titles and team environment had been achieved, it was time to determine how to implement them and to get the staff to agree. What was needed was a scheme that would promote both ideas, and reward staff for being part of it.

If we look at the 'normal' company system of rewards we find find there are basically two methods: promotion and merit bonuses. (We shall ignore company profit sharing and similar methods—discussed in Chapter 14—for the moment, as we want to focus on salary pay systems only.)

Merit bonus systems tend not to work as staff become demoralised at bonus time if they do not get one. The easy answer is for everyone to get a bonus, but that destroys any chance of the high producers and hard workers seeing any worth in the scheme. This in turn prevents the system from working and makes it an unwelcome burden on the company.

Also, it may not be possible to pay merit bonuses if the company is in financial difficulties, regardless of how well people have performed. If people have done extraordinarily well but receive nothing, it will be harder to motivate them during the next twelve months.

It is accepted that rewards may take forms other than money but most require some form of financial output from the company, and in hard times it is even more difficult to get the approval to spend funds. Hence, the best bonus scheme to promote company performance is simple: if the company makes a profit, every company member shares in it, and the opposite applies too. This is one of the quickest ways of ensuring effective peer pressure and makes 'managing' people very much easier.

Given the problems outlined above, we are left with promotion as a means to reward staff for excellent performance. The most common system in companies says that to give staff more money we must promote them, as shown in Figure 7.1.

Figure 7.1 Common promotion structure

Aspiration		**Function**
	High Salary ($)	
King of the Mountain	———┼———	Executive
Potential King	———┼———	Manager
	Company Ladder	
Aspiring King	———┼———	Supervisor
Breeding ground for Kings	———┼———	Workforce
	Low Salary	

Some of the staff in our department were only partly trained, and this training was not in the areas required. There were certain positions requiring skills that were more difficult to learn and, because they were reserved for the highest paid staff, only a limited number of employees could fill them. Moreover, the people in these positions did not want any others trained in the skills as they believed it would bring their own jobs into risk and threaten their status as Kings of the Mountain as well as adversely affecting their salaries and old reward system benefits.

Because our team had determined that a single job title was best for developing a true team environment, we needed a reward system for our area that did not require staff to step up the job-title ladder in order to be rewarded through their salary.

It is accepted that there are other types of rewards, such as letters of appreciation, days off with pay and the like, but we wanted to create a system that would attract the right people into the company and department and keep them there.

The basic attractions of most systems are:

1. The amount of remuneration offered for the hours, effort, skills, etc., required of the employee.
2. The method and likelihood of advancement within the company and reward system.
3. The ability of the individual to influence those parts of the company with which he or she comes in contact on a regular basis.

Unless these three attractions are properly addressed, there is very little point in spending time or effort on any of the other areas of people management.

As the team had decided on the single job title, the salary structure shown in Figure 7.1 was not appropriate to the team concept. Their solution to this problem was quite simple (but radical in today's companies): Take the salary scale in Figure 7.1 and lay it on its side. Place one job title to the left and create steps for salary improvements along it, as in Figure 7.2.

By using this method, members of staff would be able to remain in one job title but have their skill levels rewarded through having their salaries increased. The benefit is that the salary increase is now permanent provided the skills are maintained at the required levels.

If the minimum requirements of the department or area were achieved by the staff member, the reward would be a 'D' salary. If the staff member gained extra skills, then C, B or A could be achieved. With this basic change in the salary structures we had gained the best of both worlds. Staff could advance in salary within the one job title but promotions were still available to Manager and other senior titles via the old system.

If the staff member was suited to being a manager or higher, that path was still available up the vertical axis of the graph in Figure 7.2. However, if the staff member did not want to be or could not be a supervisor for any reason, but would develop more skills, then more salary could be earned within the one job title (see the horizontal axis on the graph).

Figure 7.2 Single job title: basic salary chart

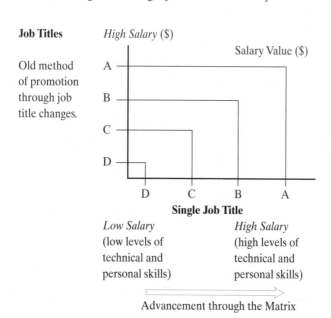

After all, not all staff want to be in the management ranks and some are just too young or have other factors restricting current or future promotion. What we achieved was the ability to reward the correct development and correct career pathing of individuals.

This was the first roughing-out of a reward system, and this step allowed all team members to understand the principle and to arrive at a consensus with regard to the direction in which we were heading .

We had combined the old and the new systems. This was much more acceptable to the company's corporate group at that time and achieved the correct end result. Remember that this is a radical change from the old ways and each area of the company must be shown the new methods and ideas in a progressive manner so they too can contribute and buy in to the change.

The Matrix Concept

This concept, which I helped to develop some years ago, is particularly suited to the notion of a single job title. When I first raised the Matrix Concept with the team, they simply asked me to go through the complete process fully. This was a result of having been through two weeks of intensive and innovative thinking. Their response was quite a change from the 'not possible' and 'it will never work here' shouts of just two weeks previously.

The concept is based on the following requirement: the department or area shall carry out only those functions and tasks which add value to the final product or service that it provides. To achieve this the department or area will only reward, through the new salary programme, those technical and personal skills developed by staff which will enable them to carry out the functions defined by the department or area (Chapter 4). This is a reward through salary only; there may be other schemes at work in the company such as a staff suggestion scheme or a profit sharing scheme.

The salary programme must aim at driving all staff to engage in only those tasks and processes which add value to the final product or service supplied to the paying customer. We do not want the customer to be told, 'Mary is on vacation for two weeks and no one can do the job but Mary, so please call back then and maybe we can take your order, fix your problem or follow up on your referral'. We do not want people in the company writing meaningless reports, moving the 'work in progress' again, waiting for signatures or approvals, and so on. The new matrix system of salary or pay focuses on eliminating such inane and soul-destroying rituals..

Up to this point, because the team was pushing on all fronts to obtain the necessary information, the following had been produced:

- Company Mission Statement
- Company Business Plan

- Department Mission Statement
- Department Business Plan
- Department Functions
- Department Tasks.

And now they had achieved the basis for a reward system.

Developing the concept further means ranking all the tasks that have been identified through the previous processes (in Chapters 4 and 5) from hardest to easiest. The hardest is put at the top of the list and easiest at the bottom. Once this is achieved the list is placed along the vertical scale of the graph or matrix. Under the old system, the vertical scale was reserved for promotions, but we created a new graph (Figure 7.3, using the tasks identified in Figure 5.1).

Taking the tasks identified earlier, the team members

grouped all the like tasks and highlighted those that were *unique* and those that were *common*:

- *Unique* were those tasks not carried out by any other section or area within the department or work location. Examples included issuing petty cash, handling customer complaints, driving or operating certain equipment.

- *Common* were those tasks carried out by all or the majority of the sections or areas within the department or work location. Examples included answering phone calls, sending telexes, using simple common tools, following procedures, being punctual.

This exercise resulted in an original list of about 140 tasks being finally reduced to eighty-five through application of unique and common task rationalization and the 'proof of the need' check.

Next the team had to decide which tasks were the hardest and which the easiest. The eighty-five tasks on the list were thus put in order with the hardest at the top and the easiest at the bottom, in accordance with their own experiences. The next day we met again and worked our way through the draft lists and moved the tasks around until partial agreement was reached. We had not achieved total agreement yet but everyone had contributed excellently to the process, and we had achieved great clarity of vision.

We applied 'proof of the need' at every stage to split some single tasks out into two or more, and grouped others.

At the end of the review five salary levels were added to the matrix along the horixontal axis (A to E). This meant the vertical axis showed tasks and the horizontal axis salary levels. No salary *amounts* were discussed and this was not the point of the exercise. The exercise was to determine what tasks would be carried out at which salary step from A to E (A being at the top), and how many salary steps would be logical, practical, and rewarding (see Figure 7.3).

The objective at this stage is to construct the matrix, not to put any real salary scales on it. If this is attempted, the issue of tasks will be lost sight of and the issue of salary levels will dominate the discussions and destroy the efforts of the team. Strong facilitator skills are required to keep the team focused.

Inserting the tasks into the matrix is fairly straightforward, but it took a lot of discussion and in some cases a lot of 'heat' was generated. It was not possible to stop this, nor would I recommend it. For all the team members to accept the end result, it is vital that all their views be heard.

It was good to see the team members begin to accept and apply logic and the 'proof of the need' check to problems. This allowed more and more emotion to be left behind and be increasingly replaced with clarity, information, and relevant experience.

Figure 7.3 Tasks inserted into the matrix

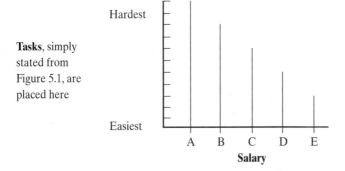

All team members were given copies of the final draft lists to take home and review again. The next day we met and adjusted the lists and determined that only four salary steps were necessary. This was now easier to do since everyone was more attuned to the objective: producing the matrix and salary steps. A strong facilitator kept the team from falling into the trap of considering *amounts* of salary and relating the salary to particular *people*. All those following this procedure will need to do the same.

The number of salary steps in the matrix is important. It determines the amount of movement available to the staff in the department and how many increases in salary or pay can occur before reaching the top. There must not be too many steps as they will become meaningless or too daunting to the staff.

The method of determining steps is a logical one. All the tasks are listed, as we have done, with hardest at the top and easiest at the bottom. Then a certain number of tasks will be allocated to the lowest salary grade, and some to the next and so on. From experience, if there are one hundred tasks in the matrix, the ratio shown in Figure 7.4 is required.

The number of tasks diminishes as the salary grade gets higher because the tasks become harder and harder. It will be much easier for a 'D' grade employee to learn how to answer the phones and handle telexes than it will be for a 'B' person to learn how to handle simultaneous train failures at three different railway stations, and solve the resulting financial problems. Both require two tasks to be learned but the amounts of learning required are clearly different.

Figure 7.4 Example of task ratios per grade

	Number of tasks	Difficulty
The first (lowest) salary grade will usually have	the first 30 to 40	easy
The next grade will usually have	the next 25 to 30	harder
The next grade will usually have	the next 15 to 20	harder
The next grade will usually have	the next 5 to 10	hardest

After further discussions the total matrix list was finally reduced to fifty-four tasks, and consensus on the final list was obtained from the complete team. This was a major victory, as there were many in the team who quite clearly stated at the beginning that the process would never work. They are now some of the strongest advocates of the process and wonder why it was never done like this before. My view is that it was quite simply never sold to them in this way before.

A car salesman I worked with in the USA for three months gave me this very important piece of advice: 'Whenever customers say no, they are not really saying no. What they are telling you is that you have not sold it to them right ... yet.' This is very true, so when your idea is instantly dismissed, think of what the salesman said and sell it another way—you will get there!

An example of a completed Skills Matrix is given in the Appendix at the end of this chapter.

Personal skills

From the Skills Matrix we can now determine the *personal skills* people must have in order to perform various *technical tasks*. If the task is to receive and send telexes, then a development list for personal skills may resemble that in Figure 7.5. (A blank reproducible form, with instructions, is reproduced opposite.)

Figure 7.5 Personal skills: development list

TASK: **Receive and send telexes**.	
Personal skills	Value
a Read/write English (in this case)	Excellent
b Ability to type	35 WPM
c Understand telex formats	Excellent
d Use abbreviations	Excellent
And so on	

Taking care of non-value-adding tasks

There is one area we must not forget. The matrix we created was of those tasks we needed to carry out in order to achieve the business plan, missions and objectives. The department or area will be performing many functions and tasks today that do not add value to the end product or service delivered to the paying customer. These functions and tasks must also be identified to enable the department's staff to take action on them.

When the matrix is constructed, it may be useful to insert these wasteful functions and tasks with a star against them indicating a need for targeting. A better method might be to list these functions and tasks separately under each unique area currently carrying them out and get the first Project Teams to work on them.

As the role of the Matrix Concept is to ensure the area concerned is carrying out only value-adding functions and tasks, it is important that this phase of task adjustment should be undertaken early by the people in the area. They are usually

PERSONAL SKILLS: DEVELOPMENT LIST

TASK:	
Personal Skills	Value

This form should be completed so that all team members know and understand what personal skills are required for each task in the matrices.

For example, in the Technical Skills Matrix (See the Appendix at the end of this chapter) if we look at Task 54 it states *Maintain a clean and orderly work area.* This would be entered at the top of the form at TASK.

Under personal skills and values could be:

Personal Skills

- All physical items are to have a designated location and be there when not in use.

- Understand the properties of cleaning materials.

- Use safety clothing and guards when at work.

- Use good husbandry sense to eliminate waste and improve the work environment.

Value

- As often as possible during working hours, and always at the end of the shift.

- All agents and substances in the working area.

- At all times.

- At all times.

best qualified to assess what to do with each non-value-adding task.

The result will be the elimination of a lot of effort, time, money and frustration spent on futile tasks. Quite often the tasks are there simply because they were inherited from decisions made in years gone by. As a simple example, telexes are often sent to addressees simply because they are in the standard message format designed years ago. One study showed a saving of $1 million if one addressee was removed from every fourth telex message. The company also saved $8500 per year simply by removing a single form.

Although some action should be taken, it is not suggested that all wasteful tasks be removed. This is because it may not be correct in all cases to dump all the non-value-adding tasks.

The team created a list of wasteful tasks and turned them over to the operators in the area unique to those tasks. The operators showed instances where some of the tasks had to be continued because other departments or areas relied on the information given. This, however, did not pass the 'proof of the need' test.

Proof of the need showed there was no need for our area to continue the task if the other area could find alternative solutions. The other areas became quite angry when they thought we were simply going to stop giving them the information. Because their ideas were as important as ours, we asked them to become involved in the team. To their disbelief, they discovered that they had all the information at their fingertips. The reports and computer systems they already had not only gave them information similar to that which they were receiving from us, but the information was more timely and accurate than we could ever supply. They had not realized this before because they had become used to the old ways of doing business and there had been no incentive to improve.

The environment in which these people worked had not been conducive to identifying and fixing wasteful practices, tasks and processes. To fix them, one has to own up to having a problem in the first place. If the company does not have an environment in which this can occur, the people cannot be blamed for not fixing problems.

If a staff member comes to you and says, 'Look, I can show where you have been wasting $3 million per year and here is my report', in the old environment the response will probably be, 'That's nice, leave it with me', and the report will then go straight into the rubbish bin. In an environment of trust and constant improvement, the response is more likely to be: 'That's great, can you find another million?'

In our case, we had been supplying the other department with the report and data sheets daily and weekly for six years

but there had never been any need to do so. The costs ran into hundreds of thousands of dollars for each of these six years. This is just one simple example of the improvements waiting around the corner for everyone who uses the system.

Constant review: adding and subtracting tasks

The type of work functions which the department or area carries out will vary from time to time and so the matrix must also be under constant review. The department may take on new functions and tasks or relinquish some. In these cases functions and tasks must be added to or subtracted from the current matrix.

No function or task can be added to or subtracted from the department without this review being carried out. All the staff will then have to be reviewed against the additions and a training schedule created. (This is explained in Chapter 12.)

This makes the Matrix Concept a complete system. With all tasks and functions under regular review it will be impossible for new work to be loaded arbitrarily on to any area of the department. With proper assessment of the tasks, the system has the ability to constantly determine the skills required for their completion. This allows the department's training, recruiting, growth and development requirements to be determined and quantified. It also ensures that skills and abilities are at a level which allows the department to meet the requirements and objectives of the customers, department, and company.

Job titles: the fat and the lean

The system of 'titles' has become firmly fixed in the workplace because the concept was promoted by organizational specialists concerned with maintaining the status quo in the job-title environment. Hence most industries have developed systems of supervision in which there is typically a ratio of one 'supervisor' to every seven to thirteen workers.

In some countries, such as Japan, this ratio has been increased to one to seventy and higher. Yet too many countries and companies can be heard saying, 'That is just not possible here' or 'That is OK for the Japanese but it could never work in this company.' I am sure there are many readers who are having similar thoughts right now.

Such a ratio may seem impossible, simply because the environment in which you work is not right. Imagine if every worker always turned up for work, always did the jobs right first time, and exceeded all your expectations; because of this the customers would be beating a trail to your company's door—and all this would be happening without supervision. Why does this not happen today?

Or, if it does, then why do you have so many supervisors? This applies to all levels in the company. Often, the CEO has six vice-presidents reporting to him or her and the VP has six general managers, each GM has six senior managers, who in turn have six departmental managers reporting to each of them, and so it goes on.

Companies have used this layered structure for centuries. Is it any wonder that anything different is seen as wrong? Most companies are 300 to 600 per cent overstaffed at management level. This fact alone makes the change to the Matrix Concept difficult for many companies, because management themselves must agree to its adoption.

If companies implemented the Matrix Concept, they would be flat rather than layered, and staff would be truly empowered to deliver the right product or service consistently to the customer and make competitive improvements to capture markets; and by creating a strong company they could be sure of keeping their jobs.

It is very clear from personal experience, interviews and information on various companies and industries that rewarding staff through salary by promotion to higher job titles is ineffective in many cases, and in fact defeats the original intention of rewarding and fostering consistently excellent performance. By promoting the people away from what, in many cases, was their area of excellence, the reward can do more harm than good.

Most existing schemes are focused on positions rather than people. Think about the structure and salary or pay programme in the company you work for.

1. Is it a programme which pays you for personal development and worth, or is it a reward or merit type scheme?
2. Does your programme establish *your* salary or that of the position?
3. Do you have a clear step-by-step map to your boss's job, as is clearly the case in the Matrix Concept?

Given good corporate leadership, promotion to different job titles can work; but it does so at some cost. Would those, with any job title, who are great producers suddenly cease to produce if they no longer had a job title but were correctly rewarded for their performance instead?

Job titles ensure company structures cannot be flattened to create environments of trust, effective communication and teamwork focused on exciting the paying customers so they willingly come back with their friends.

The system of permanently rewarding through job titles must be overhauled and updated with another system. Turning the organizational pyramid upside down is nothing more than a printer's dream of reprinting all organizational charts with the same number of titles the other way up. It is not progress. Similarly, removing five per cent of the titles does not count as effective change. These same staff will be brought back in as consultants in three to six months time—so why bother in the first place?

Summary

> We had now:
> 6. determined the need for the Matrix and the form of the Matrix itself.

This was a major stage in the work undertaken so far by the team members. It was a tangible end to a lot of effort, soul searching and major personal change. It also signalled the time to decide what kind of staff environment we had developed. It was not the normal type of team environment some companies use. It was certainly not the type seen in the company we were in. So what was it that we had achieved?

The matrix demands a single job title, or very few, in areas that have always required many titles to denote seniority and position. The team decided there was no real need for this 'tradition' and felt that the new company environment would operate better within the Matrix Concept.

There was no longer any need for numerous specialists and they were replaced by multi-skilled staff. These staff would be of more value to the company and the matrix would facilitate staff development to a degree hitherto unheard of in this area or within the company.

Appendix

Effective date: _____ / /19
Amendment Number:

TECHNICAL SKILLS MATRIX

TECHNICAL SKILL	A	B	C	D
1. Manage business to plan	x			
2. Develop final plan and adjust	x			
3. Develop contingency plans	x			
4. Negotiate with contractor & agents	x			
5. Advise senior management of prime incidents	x			
6. Assume team leader responsibilities	x	x		
7. Adjust plans				
8. Advise/liaise with other departments	x	x		
9. Interface with government agencies	x	x		
10. Ensure all staff are qualified	x	x		
11. Confirm resources available to meet operational demands	x	x		
12. Co-ordinate facilities and maintenancee of same	x	x		
13. Initiate and authorize extreme emergency recovery action	x	x		
14. Ensure schedule alterations are actioned and distributed	x	x	x	
15. Allocate training time	x	x	x	
16. Provide service recovery to customers and suppliers	x	x	x	
17. Check contractor co-ordination prior to time of customer demand	x	x	x	
18. Provide exception information	x	x	x	
19. Ensure maintenance periods are maximized and balanced	x	x	x	
20. Assign work time to resources	x	x	x	

Technical Skills Matrix contd

21. Ensure contracts are actioned and fulfilled	x	x	x	
22. Direct failure recovery and the following effort and reviews	x	x	x	
23. Obtain information for management reporting on special inquiries	x	x	x	
24. Prepare emergency package and distribute to concerned	x	x	x	
25. Monitor and maintain correct levels of support during maintenance checks	x	x	x	
26. Maintain relevant databases	x	x	x	x
27. Action signals and telexes	x	x	x	x
28. Locate missing customer details	x	x	x	x
29. Process claims and requests	x	x	x	x
30. Audit operational status sheets	x	x	x	x
31. Determine utilization of prime assets and sub-units	x	x	x	x
32. Ensure all communications are actioned during the shift	x	x	x	x
33. Implement the selected plan	x	x	x	x
34. Issue hourly report on life controlling systems as per address list	x	x	x	x
35. Constantly aim to improve the way the company does business	x	x	x	x
36. Maintain adequate records of disruptions or crisis events	x	x	x	x
37. Maintain personnel files	x	x	x	x
38. Accept and process dangerous goods meeting company limits	x	x	x	x
39. Monitor weather conditions and forward the information to appropriate departments	x	x	x	x
40. Ensure overseas requests are processed as prime concern	x	x	x	x
41. Prepare reports	x	x	x	x

Technical Skills Matrix contd

42. Print graphs and charts	X	X	X	X
43. Provide information to the customer	X	X	X	X
44. Collect fees and cash as required	X	X	X	X
45. Pay out expenses to customers if rquired	X	X	X	X
46. Ensure customer and work standards are maintained	X	X	X	X
47. Maintain employee records	X	X	X	X
48. Maintain regular contact with customers	X	X	X	X
49. Plot graphs and data sheets	X	X	X	X
50. Obtain necessary accomodation for visiting VIPs	X	X	X	X
51. Acknowledge all customer suggestions and ideas	X	X	X	X
52. Maintain clarity in work and in all shift turnovers	X	X	X	X
53. Ensure supplies are maintained	X	X	X	X
54. Maintain a clean and orderly work area.	X	X	X	X

This matrix to be used in conjunction with the Personal Skills Matrix (Chapter 8).

The tasks on this matrix are very broad, as are those in the Personal Skills matrix list, but they point to the tasks required. The details of each of these tasks will be found in the Job Performance Guide (JPG) as explained in Chapter 10.

8

The whole person

The next decisions to be made concerned the kind of people the new organization required and how we could ensure that the system of adding or replacing staff in the future maintained these criteria.

In many companies people fall into three very broad categories as described below. (These are very broad indeed, but will do for the point I want to make.)

- *People 1: Excellent all-rounders* are good at their jobs and are people-persons, that is, they get on with most people.

- *People 2: Great technical people* are good at their jobs but no one can stand them because they lack the people side of development. No one will tell them this because their technical skills are so good.

- *People 3: Great people-persons* are good with people but are no good technically. No one will tell them so because they are such great people.

Why do such diverse people groups exist in the same company? They may all have joined on the same day, at the same branch, through the same training school or with the same intention of doing the best their skills would allow.

The reason for the diversity lies in the structures within companies. Due to pressures of workload, On-Job-Training in technical skills was probably skimped or bypassed in the case of group 3 people. Perhaps the supervisor's own experiences were of the 'thrown in the deep end' variety, so he or she felt that this method would suffice for the group 2 people who came through his or her area. Some people get lucky or are extremely hard triers, and make every effort to develop both technical and people skills, and these are group 1 people. Again, this is a very *broad* look at the *end results* of many organizational systems. If they worked in the past, that simply reflects acceptance of them, but it does not necessarily mean the decisions were right. Today's inheritance (see the Introduction) is a clear indication of the disastrous results of those decisions.

Personal skills

Our team tackled the problem of how to ensure that the majority of people in the department belonged to group 1. We arrived at the solution of having not just a technical skills matrix but a personal skills matrix as well.

The *technical skills matrix* ensured that the job skills would be developed to match the tasks in the matrix, and enabled the actual tasks to be carried out correctly. (See Figure 7.5 and the Appendix at the end of Chapter 7.)

The *personal skills matrix* would ensure that the people skills were developed to meet the teamwork requirements of the new company environment. (See Figure 8.1 and the matrix following it.)

Both matrices would enable the right people for the team environment to be selected and developed today and in the future.

To this end it was necessary to determine the personal skills and attributes necessary to build the matrix. We agreed that this matrix would have four salary steps to match those in the technical skills matrix. It was also decided that to move up the salary levels, say from D to C, a staff member must advance up both matrices. This would ensure that the environment was correct for developing the whole person (People 1), and would not allow employees to develop great technical skills without people skills and vice versa.

The personal skills specifications were generated through

brainstorming by the team members. The easy way to get this conversation started was to ask each team member to describe the type of person he or she would want his or her boss to be. The lists were quite long, and confusion arose between what were technical skills and what were personal.

Then we had to rank the personal skills in order from most difficult to easiest, in exactly the same way as had been done with the the technical skills matrix task list. The chief personal skill needed is for the person joining the company to have the ability to be a 'team member'. The hardest is the ability to be a 'team leader' (see Figure 8.1).

No longer could someone be simply one-sided. Each person in the matrix system could see what technical and personal skills had to be developed in order to advance to the next salary step.

It would also be possible for someone to drop a grade if the levels previously reached were not maintained.

The personal skills were discussed and amended until they made logical sense and both the technical skills and personal skills matrices were brought in line with each other and matched to four salary steps, as shown in Figure 8.1.

Examples of 'personal skills' selected include:

- The ability to be a *team member* in order to join the department at D or any grade. It would be illogical not to have this as the first requirement for applicants to be tested against.

- The ability to *listen* is vital at C grade and above, as the staff are training others at this time and interacting more with both internal and external customers. Listening is a skill that needs coaching and must be developed and demonstrated at D grade before anyone can move to C or higher.

- The ability to develop to be *team leader* is what all the steps from D to A are about. It is the final step in the personal skills matrix. The next step or option will depend on the company's structure and whether the team member wants to move on.

The logical sense of the whole Matrix Concept process was not clear to many at the beginning for all sorts of reasons, but with the skills the team were developing in problem solving and group work it was becoming easier to talk things out. Most team members were now being much more frank for most of the time and a more relaxed atmosphere was developing. There was no longer a need to prove how clever or superior one was because the need to solve the larger task at hand had become the focal point.

Figure 8.1 Personal skills matrix

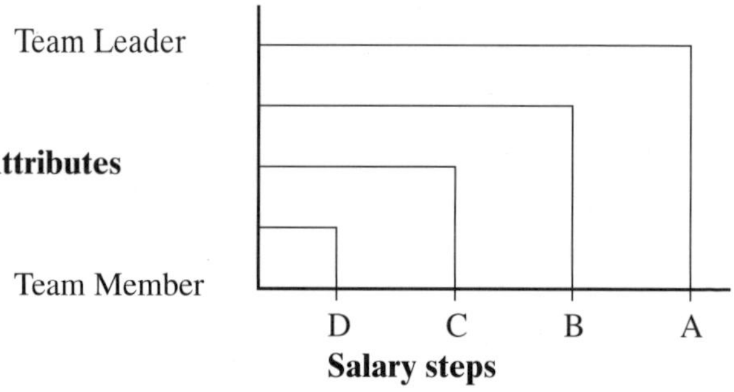

Team leader

Team leader is not a high-flying title or a level above everyone else. It refers to someone who acts like a captain in a sports team. In sports, the captain is a team member who often wears an arm band to let everyone know that he or she is carrying out an additional role but is first and foremost very much a member of the team.

In the Matrix Concept the team leader would normally be an 'A' grade in technical and personal skills. In order to satisfy all

Effective date: /   /19
Amendment Number:

PERSONAL SKILLS MATRIX
SKILL   A B C D

	A	B	C	D
1. Team leader	x			
2. Decisive	x			
3. Leadership/Followship	x			
4. Good conflict resolution skills	x			
5. Confident	x	x		
6. Clear communicator	x	x		
7. Good interpersonal skills	x	x		
8. Innovative	x	x		
9. Works well independently	x	x		
10. Quality worker	x	x	x	
11. Good planning skills	x	x	x	
12. Vigilant	x	x	x	
13. Ability to teach others	x	x	x	
14. Flexible and adaptable	x	x	x	
15. Accepts responsibility	x	x	x	
16. Achieves targets	x	x	x	
17. Willing to listen	x	x	x	
18. Able to self critique	x	x	x	x
19. Logical	x	x	x	x
20. Guided by procedures	x	x	x	x
21. Willing to learn	x	x	x	x
22. Good attitude towards authority	x	x	x	x
23. Reliable/punctual	x	x	x	x
24. Loyalty	x	x	x	x
25. Team member	x	x	x	x

This matrix to be used in conjunction with the Technical
Skills Matrix (Chapter 7)

the demands of the system, he or she must be able to function as an all-rounder.

The team leader will ensure that others in the team assume the role of team leader as part of the On-Job-Training programme and during the team leader's absence. In some teams the team leader role is naturally rotated so everyone gains from the experience of leading.

The team leader's role is not to dictate or direct the actions of the team members. It is to co-ordinate the resources available in order to achieve effectively and efficiently the best products and services for the paying customer. The most important resource is people, not robots or machinery.

The experience of assuming the role of leader (in the sense of team captain rather than the old style 'supervisor' or 'boss') fosters in each person the ability and desire to be both a team member and his or her own individual leader. The concept of team member first and own leader second produces an environment in which one team leader can lead 150 people. This is another example of how 'what may have sounded crazy before . . . is now possible'.

Summary

The weaknesses of salary programmes become evident when one talks to staff in many companies. Why someone is where he or she is today can be questioned and, importantly, even if the 'job title' reward is correct, one may ask whether he or she is really in a position to allow both the person and the company to achieve the best balance between business and personal advantage.

The total person must be developed. Failure to do so in the past may be seen as a function of the company's system, and the willingness of the company's people to operate it. If the system promotes status and climbing over others, then the system needs an overhaul. If the system does not demand that the whole person be developed so that he or she is a good team member and own-team leader, then the system needs an overhaul.

Many people in companies today would not pass the 'total person' test of the joint matrices. That is not their fault. The company systems in which they have developed have in many cases made them what they are today . So, everyone must be given a chance to change, and if they do not, they will not be welcome in the new environment.

We had now:

7. determined the need for a personal skills matrix and determined the roles of team leaders

---

9

People

Staffing and skills in the new system

With the initial matrices now completed it was time to look at how to put the Matrix Concept in place and how to determine the correct staff numbers and skills required by it. Inevitably, this was the time when many of the old ways of doing business and old habits reappeared among the team members.

We had already achieved great team unity by the end of the second week and members were quickly adjusting to each other as team members. It was rewarding to see the clarity of purpose with which the team members had created the two matrices. This was because the particular task of matrix development did not require the questioning of staff levels or people too often.

The next step in the process was kept as clinical and unemotional as possible, for most of the team members had never been through such a step before. Now was the time for strong facilitation, and the need to stress the importance of the application of logic, and the importance of keeping our aims clearly in mind.

We first listed the following on the whiteboard:

- shift patterns
- people's names
- their current 'expertise'
- their job title
- their current level in the department

(Use of the whiteboard and flip charts allowed everyone to focus on the same information at once.)

This led to discussion about the people numbers, skills and so on required in the new matrix system. We had to tackle the question of what the department *should* be doing. So both the *present work* and the *right work* had to be considered: the present work to see how that was handled, and the right work to see what changes to the existing structure and people levels were needed.

The discussions were long and hard. Examples of the major problems encountered were:

1. The area that was to lose the most staff fought the hardest. Their argument was: 'This area is the busiest and that is why we have the most people, and why there can be no changes here.' This argument was a hangover from past ways of thinking. 'Proof of the need' was thus applied: Is the area the busiest because it is doing what it should be doing, or busy only because it is doing what it has always done? This check enabled the process to regain its focus. (One company I know eliminated a total of 60 per cent of all tasks in one whole department once this clarity of purpose had been achieved. Another removed 80 per cent of tasks from an area. Both had thought they could not make any changes when they began the process.)

2. Another argument raised was: 'It takes years to learn these skills so we must retain all the staff in that area just to cover the day-to-day work.' There is some truth in this statement, but time also allows the growth of specialists. These are the people who 'know more and more about less and less'. We were no longer looking for specialists, but rather for staff who were multi-skilled and could be effective as part of a team. Specialists were required previously for two main reasons: (1) many of the jobs had become more complex as they developed through the adding-on of tasks; (2) the 'job title' environment condoned the portrayal of roles within the company as complicated so that jobs could be split into two or three parts and more job titles created.

However, by maintaining clarity of purpose the team members' resistance to people changes began to be broken down. They were really using 'people' as an excuse, because although no one said it initially, they could see that this process was breaking up what they thought were their individual empires. That is what makes this part of the process so very hard, and the facilitator must be aware of this, keep everyone focused on the end goal, let people talk, and make them listen. Empathy rather than sympathy is required.

Empathy can be illustrated by the following story: A fire extinguisher salesman called on a house and found a man sitting outside, with his head in his hands. When the salesman enquired whether he would like an extinguisher, the man let loose with: 'My wife is in the hospital for an operation, my son has just written off my car and my other son has broken his leg on a skiing holiday and I have to collect him and I have no way of doing it, so I don't need one of those right now!' The salesman went straight past the man and started to screw an extinguisher onto the wall in the kitchen. The man asked, 'Didn't you hear what I said to you?', and the salesman replied, 'Yes I did, and with all those things going on in your life right now, the last thing you need is for your house to burn down.'

Shedding the past and the ownership mentality

We had to determine how many people would be required in the new structure, how the transition could be accomplished, and how long that transition period would be.

No one owned anything now except accountabilities, and the team members had to be reminded regularly of that. A flaw in organizations today is that management are taught they own certain assets including people, territory and goals within the organization. Many meetings are held to discuss why one department did something in another's area. These meetings are preceded by letters and memos chastizing the intruder or offender. The fact that the offender was taking care of the

customer at the time is seen as unimportant. The lesson learnt by the offending staff member is to leave the customer alone in future and clearly state, if challenged, that it is not his or her job or area of responsibility.

All staff, especially management, have to be retrained to see that they own nothing, and that everyone should be working towards the company's goals and serving the customer. Territories and other barriers, monthly reports, job descriptions, formal organizational structures, and job titles all add to the ownership mentality. The entire company and all its staff suffer when the paying customer quietly walks off to the competition.

Rather than owning anything, people in the company are there 'to reliably provide a quality product or service at the right price to the paying customers so they will come back willingly and will refer people they know'. (Keep saying this, and more and more of your people will think it and believe it.)

It was absolutely necessary for all the team members to give up the protectionist arguments they had developed and held to be true over the years. In past staffing budget exercises, the norm was simply to argue for every position you currently had and to try to get even more. It was an exercise in empire building. The team had to shed the past and the sort of decisions which had produced the staff levels in place at the start of the review.

The team had some very long discussions before the old ways of judging staffing requirements were shaken sufficiently to allow them to start down the path of determining the department's new structure.

The need for multi-skilling

Each team member stated what he or she had decided would be the new staff levels in his or her area and explained how this number had been arrived at. According to the Matrix Concept, it is not the number of specialists that counts but the number of people who can be multi-skilled to carry out only those tasks which the matrix process identifies as adding value to the final product or service.

In the department under consideration there were originally four groups of specialists and in the end, after applying the matrix logic and 'proof of the need' checks, there were none.

Usually in a department or area, there are those with specialist skills who enjoy working there more than others. This is natural and expected and should not be held against them. However, these same people, through cross-training, will:

- have a better understanding of the total department
- have a better understanding of others' work and workloads
- make decisions based on better knowledge of the business

- be able to support others as workloads vary, and remove the overburden at peak times in other areas
- be able to train others in multiple functions and tasks
- alleviate support staff shortages due to sickness, vacations, and the like.

All the above can be achieved because the Matrix Concept is a structured system that does not leave things to one manager, and does not fail because of workloads being too great in one area. The system is habitual and permanent, and will continue to work even though individuals may leave their jobs. What matters is the number of cross-trained or multi-skilled staff required to carry out the total functions and tasks in a particular area.

This number depends on many factors, but the basics are:

- the type and volume of work
- the activities at various times of the day (workload)
- the types of skill required at these times
- the spread of the peaks and troughs
- the hours of activity (twenty-four hours a day)
- the number of days in the week required
- the seasonal impacts.

Initially the workload drives the study. Collecting the necessary data was not hard, as the department, like so many others, had continued to produce the monthly reports that no one usually ever dealt with. These gave data, rather than real information, concerning workloads under the old structure. This data was necessary to help establish roughly how much would be changed.

The team also collected a lot of information about the real workplace, future projects, and coming changes. The result was a very large reduction in workloads for the department. The skills of specialists could be partially replaced by check sheets and the rest by multi-skilling the staff. This was the first real breakthrough, as the team began to see that there was no longer any need for everyone to be specialists.

The clear definition of precisely which functions and tasks were value-adding led to the elimination of considerable amounts of work. There was a need in the end for one specialist—quite a change from ninety. This was the first real sign, only three weeks after the establishment of the team, that the walls would at last come tumbling down.

Almost all the work of the team was carried out on a whiteboard, and this allowed everyone the freedom to alter the flow charts and tables and to experiment. Team members took turns explaining their views on staff levels until there was a mess on the board which was somehow to be the new plan. This first attempt was loaded with everyone's personal wants and the staff numbers arrived at were wrong, simply because it was a first attempt. Using the newly developed logic everyone knew we could do much better.

The process then went on to the stage at which team members shoot down everyone else's suggestions while protecting their own. Everyone recalled many past experiences including all the possible disasters that could occur if one staff member was moved to another area or taken away, or if multi-skilling was introduced and so on. This is not a bad sign. If someone is willing to discuss or argue, then they are thinking. The earlier successes in developing the matrices arose from the fact that people and empires were not critically affected. Now, if staff were to be regrouped, a management staff member risked having fewer than the required ten staff under him or her, which would mean loss of position, empire, job title, and maybe even salary. Thus there was a tendency for individuals to fight to keep what they had.

The key role of the facilitator at this stage is to keep everyone focused on the goal of determining the people levels needed to meet the requirements of the matrix. The goal was not to decide what was going to happen to specific management jobs. It was not and never is mandatory that the facilitator be someone from outside of the company. Look around your company and you will find many good people who can do the job or who could do it after some training.

Right-sizing

The first attempts of the team produced about a 10 per cent cut in numbers. The second attempt got us up to 15 per cent and here we froze for some time. The talks continued until proof of the need logic at last enabled us to make a breakthrough which pushed the reduction up to 37 per cent. This was a brutal cut in people numbers and there were still some reservations. The cuts were reduced to 35 per cent to give the group a little 'win' and protection (see Figure 9.1).

The whole focus of the Matrix Concept is not to achieve staff reductions or staff increases, but to determine the *correct* people levels through the application of logic and information about what value-adding workloads the department or area must achieve.

In many cases the staff reductions (when these occur) are in the region of 20 per cent, but there are also cases of increases and they have tended to be in the order of 12 per cent. (These figures are given to show what has happened in areas where the Matrix Concept has been applied, and not to guide anyone's thinking. Each and every case is different. To say otherwise would be neither logical nor based on any facts pertaining to your particular company, department, or area.) The process of the Matrix Concept is to take each area through a set-by-step application of logic and 'proof of the need' checks and let the missions, goals and workloads determine the end result. It is in no one's best interest to guess how it will come out. A British study shows that attempts at best-guessing the answer at the beginning of a project were proved to be totally wrong 90 per cent of the time.[1]

1. 'Best guessing the answer by managers' was reported by consultants at a meeting in New Zealand: up to 90 per cent of British managers guessed a different answer to the one actually selected by projects teams who undertook to solve the same problem.

So it is a process for neither down- nor up-sizing, but for *right-sizing*. Some areas, like our team's department, achieved a reduction that was quite substantial. Why was the area so overstaffed? Again the answer is so very simple: The management decisions of the past had established the department structure, staffing, work, and ways of doing work. This process sets about shedding those past management decisions and their results, one of which, in the majority of cases, is overstaffing at all levels within companies. (See Figure 9.2)

If any company has people who are experts in certain functions and tasks for which the company no longer has any need, the end result in many cases is that people are retained because 'that's how we do business around here', or they are assigned another job title, whether needed or not.

Figure 9.1 Right-sizing stages

Attempts	Staff Reduction
1st Discussion focused on specialists and how badly they are needed.	10%
2nd Discussion focused on multi-skilling and the benefit that would bring. The more multi-skilling people have, the more valuable they are to the company. The broader the range of tasks they can do, the fewer the number of people needed. The system would need a reward/salary system to complement this.	15%
3rd At this stage the team felt that even more people could be removed from the department. They gained an understanding of the Matrix Concept's real effectiveness in empowering people to take charge of their futures.	37%

All companies must face the fact that if the function or tasks are not to be carried out, the company cannot afford to keep a person in that role. Moving the person to another department for the sake of convenience will adversely affect the receiving department's staff. The company must make a decision to right-size.

Figure 9.2 Samples of the impact of multi-skilling

Relating to staff:	**Population**
• If all are multi-skilled • if some are partly multi-skilled • with no multi-skilling	X X + 23% X + 46%

The Matrix Concept drives all areas of the company by way of a system that defines precisely which actions add value to the product or service that the customer is willing to buy. If the task or role does not fit this process, it should be eliminated or reduced to a minimum. This does not necessarily mean that the company is overstaffed. It could mean the people are simply not in the right places, doing the right things.

The team had decided that there was a need for only 65 per cent of the main work group's original staff. This is surprising as there had recently been a review of the department by the Industrial Organization Group and their findings were that staffing should be increased by 10 per cent to enable the department to operate efficiently.

The team reviewed their decision and decided that a further two per cent were required to cover vacations and days off.

It is worth noting that the size of a company is not a consideration when determining whether or not to tackle the problem of restructuring. Size only influences the time it will take to achieve the first transitional stage. So *just do it*.

Figure 9.3 describes the method of changing a company in order to meet and exceed customer expectations effectively and efficiently. It is an excellent method of shedding the past.

Figure 9.3 Proven steps for best results

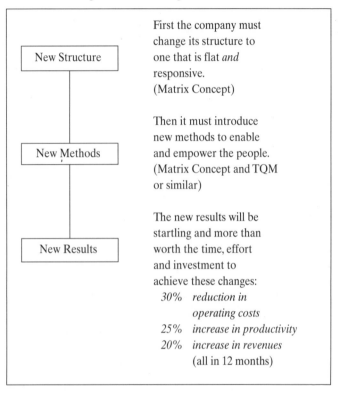

First the company must change its structure to one that is flat *and* responsive.
(Matrix Concept)

Then it must introduce new methods to enable and empower the people.
(Matrix Concept and TQM or similar)

The new results will be startling and more than worth the time, effort and investment to achieve these changes:

30%   reduction in operating costs
25%   increase in productivity
20%   increase in revenues
(all in 12 months)

Once the tough decision to change is made, further transition will become normal and expected provided the change is focused on how the company does business; that is, focused on the methods and not on who owns what.

Summary

The Matrix Concept focuses on *value-adding work* and *people*.

It allows the company to be restructured so that:

1. The main effort and rewards are directed towards gaining and maintaining customers.
2. Value is added to training and to steps of the process.
3. Market share is increased, with effective margins.
4. The company is strengthened.

As the team discovered, the management decisions of the past have placed the wrong numbers of people with the wrong skills in the wrong places. In implementing the Matrix concept there will be many changes. Whole departments may go and others may be formed through efforts directed at the four results listed above. There will always be changes to 'the way the company does business'.

The staff reductions could easily have been staff increases. The process puts emphasis first on doing the right tasks right, first time. It then uses these results to determine the right number of people and the skills they will require. The Matrix Concept thus places emphasis on the whole person.

It also requires management to be visionary and inspired. They are the ones who have made the decisions in the past and they must make the new decisions for today and the future.

We had now:
8. determined the staff numbers and skills required

10

Job Performance Guide

Everyone in the department needs to know what is expected for each of the matrix tasks. The tasks are detailed in just a few words which give an indication of the task to be carried out (see Figure 5.1 and the Technical Skills Matrix at the end of Chapter 7). However, everyone also needs to know what steps must be taken in order to accomplish the task. It is important that the steps for each task in the matrix are clearly established and known for many reasons, the main ones being:

- to set a base standard
- to encourage constant improvements to the work
- to allow everyone to know the content of the work
- to allow everyone to know what to train for
- to enable self-learning.

As is evident from the Technical Skills Matrix at the end of Chapter 7, the tasks are simply stated as short headings. This is for simplicity and ease of use as the matrix must be customer friendly and the customers are the company's own people. If the people are clear about what is expected of them, they will be better able to provide the customer with the right product or service, and both the company and its people will reap the benefits.

For each task listed in the matrix a Job Performance Guide (JPG) is created *by the staff* in the area of the task. If more than one area carries out the same task, then a member from each area will contribute to a single JPG, or if the same task is handled quite differently by multiple areas within the same department, each area would create its own JPG (see Figure 10.1).

From Figure 10.1 it is clear that there are *no time limits* placed against the tasks: no minutes, hours or days by which each step should be completed. This is not the purpose of the JPG; rather, the *purpose* is to list clearly and in sequence the steps involved in actually carrying out the task. It is a way of explaining the task accomplishment and not a time-and-motion standard against which everyone will be compared.

The JPG starts with a 'trigger' question: What must happen for it to be necessary for the task to be carried out? This question alone will cause a few hairs to turn grey.

Figure 10.1 Job Performance Guide (JPG)

Last Updated:

Area of work: _____		
This task is:_____		
1. Each Matrix task to have a JPG created. 2. The JPG to be created by the staff doing the task. 3. The JPG to: • start: from when the task is triggered • finish: when does one know it is complete?		
Step	Task steps	Remarks

The JPG is continued step by step until the final step is reached for each task. The final step should clearly state how the person carrying out the task will know it is completed: see Figure 10.1 and the Appendix at the end of this chapter.

The speed at which the task is accomplished depends very much on its difficulty, the frequency with which it is carried out, the person's physical aptitude and familiarity with the task, and many other factors. If the company sets targets for the speed of doing tasks, quality will suffer—it always does. Many people will take short cuts which can result in poorer quality, less productivity, and higher costs, as illustrated by the following story:

> A restaurant was attracting more and more customers with its special cakes. When the chef went on holiday for three weeks a temporary chef took over. This person continued to meet the increasing demand for the cakes for the first ten days, but then demand started to fall off. By the time the original chef came back demand was down to less than half of what it had been and was continuing to drop off. Management had thought there must be competition in the market-place and to combat this they had even dropped their prices, but that brought no real improvement.
>
> The original chef returned and tasted the cakes and found them poor in all respects, except that they still looked like her originals. The temporary worker cheerfully explained how he had found ways of making the cakes faster and much more cheaply than before. There were savings in mixture (using alternative substances), costs (the oven was on for shorter periods), and productivity was up (he could produce more in the same period). He thought that the fact that fewer and fewer cakes were selling meant that there was market competition, not that the cakes weren't good to eat.

Was the temporary chef wrong? Didn't he meet all the 'normal' business criteria of increased speed, lower costs and higher productivity? It is desirable that processes within the company be carried out in a shorter time frame, at lower costs, with improved productivity, but that does not mean speeding up the assembly line or driving people harder and harder with shorter

and shorter deadlines. These methods will almost certainly mean fewer and fewer customers as time progresses, because companies can only apologize so much before customers depart for good.

JPGs as business tools

The JPGs are excellent means of stating how tasks are carried out, but they are also excellent business tools for:

- evaluating the work content
- improving the processes of the company
- On-Job-Training (OJT)
- self-learning.

(Training and self-learning will be explained in Chapter 12.)

The ability to evaluate the work content and improve the processes is vital and meets two of the requirements mentioned above: speeding up the processes and reducing response time.

If we look at the task 'Produce the monthly report' with a very simple JPG, we will be able to demonstrate the excellent business effect of the JPG (see Figure 10.2).

The before and after positions are shown below: i.e. *before* the process was understood and 'proof of the need' applied and *after*.

The changes were determined not by 'management' but rather by all members working together to ensure that the processes being carried out were adding value.

Figure 10.2 shows how the process was first discovered. *Discovered* is a valid term because most tasks are carried out through habitual practices in many, many cases rather than through understanding. So realizing what is really happening today is a discovery, and thereafter improvements will begin. It is important to understand the process, and flow charting is an excellent method of drawing the picture.

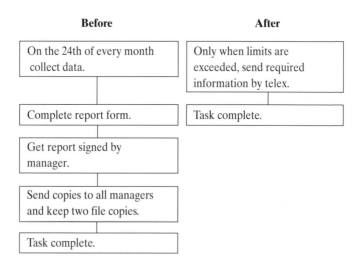

Before

| On the 24th of every month collect data. |

| Complete report form. |

| Get report signed by manager. |

| Send copies to all managers and keep two file copies. |

| Task complete. |

After

| Only when limits are exceeded, send required information by telex. |

| Task complete. |

Figure 10.2 Job Performance Guide
(how the task is carried out today)

Last Updated: **12/12/19.**

	Area of work: **XYZ Area**

This task is: **Produce the monthly report**

1. Each Matrix task to have a JPG created.
2. The JPG to be created by the staff doing the task.
3. The JPG to:
   - start: from when the task is triggered
   - finish: when does one know it is complete?

Step	Task steps	Remarks
1	On 24th of every month collect the following data: • Budget/actuals/variances • Staff/sickness/productive hours • Earnings/contracts completed	Formats in 'Master Forms' File.
2	Complete the monthly report format and have it signed by the Department Manager.	
3	Send copies to all Managers and keep two copies in the 'Monthly Report File'.	Addresses in the cover of the file.
4	When completed report is filed the task is complete.	Complete.

If this series of steps is questioned at each stage, we will be able to determine 'proof of the need' and the value-adding ability of each step. Let's go through all four steps:

1. *On the 24th of the month collect the data stated.*

Proof of the need:
Upon questioning the date, it was found that most departments varied as to the period covered in the reports and therefore the data submitted was just that—data, not information. The date was not important either, as the internal customer (recipient) wanted the report only when certain limits had been exceeded.

If there was 'No exceeding', there should be 'No report'. Since 30 per cent of the data was already reported by other departments it was eliminated from this department's reports.

2. *Complete the monthly report format and have it signed by the manager.*

Proof of the need:
The chief recipient of the report was asked to comment on its content and format. He claimed that half the remaining 70 per cent of data reported was of no use to him and should have been in a different format. A telex of the true 'information' would have been sufficient.

There was no need for the manager to sign the report as the information was obtained from charts held in the office, and telex formats required no signatures.

3. *Send copies to all managers and keep two copies in the Monthly Report File.*

Proof of the need:
Of the managers receiving the report only two said they actually needed it. It was then discovered that the genuinely relevant information was in the computer systems in those two requesting areas but no one had ever shown the managers how to access it.

Keeping two copies in the file was a hangover from a

supervisor who had left the department seven years earlier. The data could be called out of the computer systems at any time, and the wall charts were printouts from the computer, so the need for copies was eliminated.

4. *When the completed report is filed the task is complete.*

No longer applies!
The JPG could now be rewritten since the bureaucratic and non-value-adding steps and actions had been removed (see Figure 10.3).

Figure 10.3 Job Performance Guide (improved to what should be carried out)

Last Updated: **21/12/19.**

Area of work: **XYZ Area**

This task is: **Produce the monthly report**

1. Each Matrix task to have a JPG created.
2. The JPG to be created by the staff doing the task.
3. The JPG to:
   • start: from when the task is triggered
   • finish: when does one know it is complete?

Step	Task steps	Remarks
1.	**Only** when limits are exceeded send the following information: • Variances and causes. • Productive hours. • Contracts completed, status of other contracts.	Format on signal screen. For the full month just prior to occurrence.
2.	Send information by signal. The task is complete.	Addressees on Format.

By looking at value-adding and customer service the following had been achieved:

1. The task was shortened by approximately 60 per cent, and there was only the occasional instance when the limits were exceeded.
2. There was consequently an increase in the rate at which the task can be completed (a productivity gain).
3. There was a reduction in the quantity of materials and assets used.
4. Less time was wasted.
5. Old reports were no longer held 'just in case' they were needed.
6. Systems used to collect the information were also overhauled as a follow-on project. Because the report was compiled *only* when the agreed limits were exceeded, computer time devoted to its collation and production was reduced by 90 per cent.

If there were no cases of exceeding the agreed limits, then no reports would be sent during the whole year. *That would equate to a 100 per cent improvement* in all areas and would allow the customer to concentrate time, effort and resources where they are really needed.

It must be stressed there is still no mention of the *time* required to do the task in the JPG but simply a removal of the bureaucratic and non-value-adding steps (in this case unnecessary reports and data not needed by the customer). The internal customer then has a clearer sense of what information is needed to provide timely, high quality support to his or her external customers.

Making the changes

Who carried out these investigations and customer interviews? Not management. It was the people doing the actual work and working within the matrix system who carried the whole process out from start to finish. They had to keep the management informed, and at the end of the study, following agreed problem-solving processes, they made a presentation of their findings and recommendations to management.

Following the successful 'sale' of their project, all the changes were implemented and their Project Team took on the next task for evaluation and improvement. Success breeds success and it was great to be a part of the whole change.

If companies attempt to increase production rates by increasing the production line speeds, they will achieve only worse results. Remember:

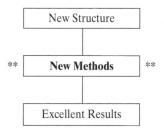

'New methods' means taking those who are the experts at the tasks—the ones doing them—and empowering them to follow through the Matrix Concept to eliminate wasteful actions, bureaucratic steps, and non-value-adding steps.

The people

People are a factor long overlooked by management until their importance has become almost a 'lost secret'. To accomplish the results detailed in Figure 10.3 required no new technology or high-cost solution. The fault lay with people who were not directed towards value-adding effort and the retention of paying customers but were directed instead towards improving too many processes through technology. These people can be just as big a burden as those people who do not want to change anything. The problem and its solution always lie with people.

Be ready, though, for *constant improvements*. Many, many times this phrase appears in books, articles, mission statements, goals, and pep talks from management—so much so that it can become tiresome for everyone. Yet the Matrix Concept not only makes it real but makes it mandatory in its operation.

As stated at the beginning of this chapter, all staff are trained against the matrices and they can also self-learn all the tasks in the matrix in their own time. The JPGs ensure that a constant methodology is used to carry out each task, and to provide a standard in terms of which to assess all staff: (Assessment is explained in the next chapter.)

Thus every staff member will have a copy of the matrices and will work his or her way through the tasks and JPGs on the road to multi-skilling. This means every staff member will be studying, reviewing, questioning and amending the JPGs on an almost daily basis. No one person will be reviewing the complete Technical Skills Matrix, but with staff developing at various levels of the matrix, most of the matrix will receive almost constant attention.

The Matrix Concept is very much geared to self-learning. Training departments can be substantially reduced in size in the area of technical skills training, but this is subject to the creation of a 'self-learning centre'. The self-learning centre enables people to study and grow at their own pace and allows time for questioning 'the way the company does business'. In most cases these centres are at departmental rather than central locations.

Amendments

To ensure control of the matrices and JPGs, amendments must be effected through an established system in which one or more people are accountable for amendment updating and for informing everyone in the department. It is also vital that the amendments are researched through some problem-solving system which allows for correct levels of discussion and analysis to prove the need for the change.

This same person or people should carry out a six- or twelve-monthly review to ensure all JPGs are being maintained. Many staff will pencil in 'typo' corrections or minor corrections to figures and the like, which must be updated too.

If the department takes on a new function or task, or a function or task is eliminated from the department, the following must occur in all cases:

1. Take on a new function or task:

The function must be broken down into tasks as explained in Chapters 4 and 5. The tasks must be compared to the existing matrices and it must be determined whether or not they are new. If there are new tasks, they must be inserted into the correct matrix at the appropriate place.

All departmental staff must be evaluated against the changes, and those at higher skill levels must be trained as soon as possible (in the next one or two months or sooner). Those staff not at the skill level where the changes occurred will be trained or will self-learn as they progress through the matrix.

As part of the empowerment process, the staff concerned must help to evaluate the impact on: the department and its teamwork, workloads, financial impacts, staff numbers, abilities required, salary variation, etc.

2. Eliminate an existing function or task:

The function must be broken down into tasks as explained in Chapters 4 and 5. Determine whether the tasks are completely or partially removed, and correct the matrix at the appropriate places.

As part of the empowerment process, the staff concerned must help to evaluate the impact on: the department and its teamwork, workloads, financial impacts, staff numbers, abilities required, salary variation, etc.

The system is very simple and is easily maintained at departmental levels. The department's management and those who work within the matrix system are the best people to maintain it. (This brings into question the need for departments like Corporate Human Resources and similar.)

Whenever there is a substantial amendment (other than 'typos', etc.) each departmental member must be given the amended matrix with an indication as to the task(s) or JPG(s) which have been amended.

The people who work within the matrix system must ensure that they are up to date with changes and must aim to constantly improve the functions, tasks, and processes. This is to enable the people in the company to deliver reliably products and services that meet the expectations of customers and will make them come back willingly, bringing with them people they know.

Management's function is to ensure that the system is being followed, that all departmental staff are self-learning and being trained against the matrices, to coach and encourage directed risks and innovations, and to carry out the assessments of people against the matrices and JPGs.

Processes

Processes are the linking of more than one step in a JPG or of more than one task. Everything we do is a process: from getting up in the morning and getting ready for work to travelling to the beach, carrying out work, and so on. The Matrix Concept builds into the organization a system to constantly and habitually improve all processes.

Most often process improvements will be the subject of teamwork, and it is important that the environment at work should be conducive to teamwork. Teamwork means doing things together to achieve a better end result than could be achieved by one individual. This is team synergy.

Summary

While the Matrix Concept seems to be focused on 'tasks', it is really directing effort at improving the processes of doing value-adding work. Its 'drivers' are:

- ensuring processes, functions and tasks are customer-directed and value-adding
- constantly eliminating non-value-adding functions, tasks, and steps, or minimizing them
- constantly improving the company's 'way of doing business'
- improving ROI, current ratio, and other key business indicators

but never leaving any part of the whole work process to wallow in the mire called 'the status quo'.

The JPGs are the ideal vehicle for exposing all the steps in all tasks and the matrix system drives and expects all departmental staff to constantly improve every one of these. It involves working with customers and people from other areas, departments, stations or companies towards improving the work processes. This also promotes broader knowledge of the business and directs all efforts at business improvements through improving quality, responsiveness, and margins.

We had now:
9. determined the need for the tasks and, through the staff, determined the resultant JPGs for all tasks

---

Appendix

Job performance Guide

Last Updated: /   /

Area of work: _____

This task is:

_____

1. Each Matrix task to have a JPG created.
2. The JPG to be created by the staff doing the task.
3. The JPG to:
   • start: from when the task is triggered
   • finish: when does one know it is complete?

Step	Task steps	Remarks

11

Assessment of people

Once the matrices were completed and the right levels of staff and skills were determined, it was time to assess existing and potential departmental people against these criteria. It was expected that many of the people currently employed would fail to measure up against the new criteria.

Purpose of the assessments

The purpose of the assessments is not to be critical of anyone or for the assessment to be used as a stick with which to intimidate. It is to evaluate individual performance and ability against the matrices, so as to make management better able to direct the individual's training in the next six months. And it will enable the individual to achieve 'value-adding' training during that time. This brings enjoyment into the workplace as all members know what is expected of them and in what respects they, as individuals, must improve.

This does not detract from the team environment but actually enhances it constantly. The skills training each individual needs comes from fellow workers as On-Job-Training (explained in Chapter 12). Thus an environment is created for both the individual and the team, and it develops quickly.

In our team's review, it was found that the company had people who had been groomed by the old environment and demands. The previous company systems had created the type of people within it. Its environment was characterized by the attitudes of:

- don't rock the boat
- do only what you are told

- check your mind in at the door and collect it on the way home
- this is your area, your phone, your job.

The staff were perceived as being there only to work the eight hours and do 'the best they can in these conditions'. Lack of interest by management made failure to perform acceptable.

In such companies, there is usually a great deal of over-production, inventory, rework, waiting around, overburdening, and the like. The staff try to change things and to do things differently, only to find the management does not listen. Management then lays the blame on the 'hourly worker', and phrases heard often include: 'they don't work hard enough', 'they should have done better', 'I used to do this or that when I was in their position', 'they seem to take delight in messing up' ('they' being the hourly workers).

Given such an environment, it would not be rational to say that, as we are now entering a new era requiring a new system, a new multi-skilling, and a team environment, only those who can fit in *immediately* will be kept.

We were making a breakthrough. The team was willing to shed the past and its poor results and to take the first major steps towards team building, true empowerment of people and previously unheard of business improvements.

Assessments

So how would the assessments be carried out and what would be important in selecting the appropriate and most suitable people? It was likely that no one would initially be perfectly suited.

It was agreed that all staff in the department must be assessed against the new criteria—the matrices—and they would from then on operate totally within the matrix system. The word 'department' is used because even though the whole company would implement the same Matrix Concept eventually, department management and staff must first carry out the whole process internally. Some departments will have more than one matrix. Some might merge or build one matrix in line with another department's as the stepping stones of development are constructed across the company.

Our team had constructed the Technical Skills Matrix and the Personal Skills Matrix, but it had yet to be decided which was more important at this initial stage. The Personal Skills Matrix is very important, as it is easier to teach technical skills than change someone's personality. Thus the Personal Skills Matrix was given greater 'weighting'.

It was now time to assess all members of the department. This was difficult for some management to do: we were talking about old friends, neighbours, fellow trainees from years back, and new recruits brought on board just six months ago.

And it was difficult because the time had come to deal with real people. This is the stage at which the management in many companies have been found wanting in the past; the proof lies in the state of today's businesses and economies. If fellow management have to be thinned out, it is easier just to maintain the status quo than make the decisions whereby friends, buddies and co-workers have to leave the department and possibly the company. When senior management are looking for traditional cost savings, the axe regularly falls on the hourly workers or their immediate supervisors. But if someone has the nerve to show how these same savings could be made throughout all levels of management, protectionism rises up at levels normally associated with mothers defending their threatened infants.

It is only when the slash-and-burn policy directly affects a senior manager or executive that the reality of what these same senior managers are doing to the people of the company hits home. The problem with slashing staff numbers and burning the salaries back is the simple fact that it is all viewed in terms of numbers. It is not personal except to the people directly affected. Companies must turn away from this very old technique that has more failures to its credit than successes.

Because it relies on people the Matrix Concept is not impersonal. The whole focus of this system is on:

- people development
- each person's right to self-improvement through the matrix steps
- the company's efforts to reach corporate goals
- the quality and price of the product or service delivered to the paying customer.

A team of management and team leaders must carry out the staff assessments, and it is the Assessment Team's judgement of each person's technical and personal skills, along with the levels attained and the results of written or practical exams, that will determine the assessed level of each person (see Figure 11.1).

Remember, the purpose of the assessment is to evaluate individual performance and ability against the matrices, so as to make management better able to direct the individual's next six months of training. The assessment is for the betterment of staff, and this will result in better products and service delivered to the customer thereby creating a stronger company.

The matrix system extends to lower levels of assessment than most other systems and has the ability to be easily used at departmental level. This is not a 'corporation doing it to you' system, but a very personal, departmental process of developing:

- people, and
- all aspects of 'the way the company does business'.

These have proven to be simply the two most important aspects of successful businesses.[1]

The system is not based on broad Position Descriptions (PDs) or Job Descriptions (JDs) which give a broad brush

1. The two most important aspects of successful business: companies stating these include Toyota (worldwide), Federal Express (USA), Xerox (England), Southwest Airlines (USA), Interlock (New Zealand).

Figure 11.1 Assessment process flow chart

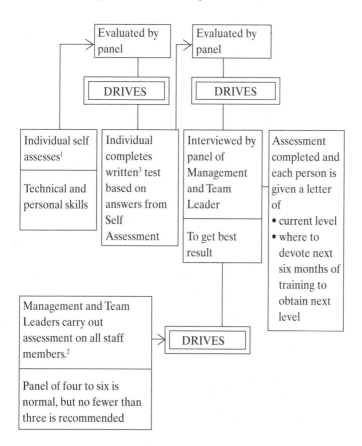

1. Individual starts here.
2. Management start here.
3. Written test and/or practical test could be used.

description of intent covered in three, five or eight paragraphs. Instead it is based on the real and actual tasks which add value to the final service or product being delivered to the paying customer and which can be defined and, in almost all cases, measured. They are measured to determine the reliability with which consistent quality is delivered, and if something is measured it can most certainly be improved.

Carrying out assessments

The assessments should be completed at least twice per year: the six-month assessment is extremely valuable for directing training and development for the next six months and so on.

The carrying out of the assessments requires the Assessment Team (AT) to be selected and to agree on the method to be used along with the time frame required to complete the full process, as shown in Figure 11.1.

The AT should be made up from the department or area's people, including:

- those managers who work frequently with the people to be assessed and who are their peers or seniors
- the Team Leaders from the same area, including the Team Leader of the person being assessed
- direct supervisors (in the old company structure) who share regular working time with the person to be assessed.

The assessment forms and procedures are discussed and agreed on, to ensure that they are up to date and in line with all changes that have occurred during the last six months. This will require the process to commence usually two months before the date by which the assessments should be completed.

Stage 1

The updated assessment forms are handed out to all the people who are to be assessed. With the forms will be guidelines on wording and methods to be used, and the process which will be followed over the next two months. This will already have been explained to everyone in the department prior to the assessment. The team environment will enable this topic to be discussed just like any other.

The assessment form can consist of the two matrices (Technical Skills and Personal Skills) with a score range at the base. Each person allocates points alongside those areas in which he or she feels he or she has some capability. Weighting might occur, depending on the importance of the technical or personal skill. Those areas in which no knowledge or experience has been gained would be left blank (see Figure 11.2).

Figure 11.2 Assessment form: simple style

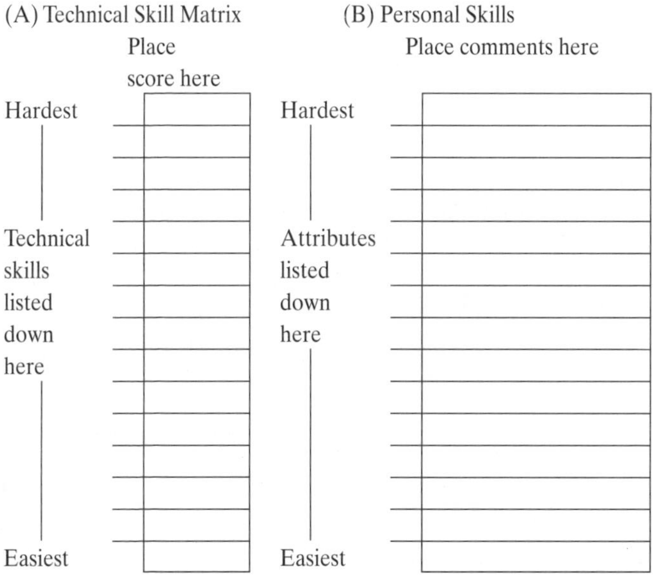

Note: The Personal Skills must be evaluated in words rather than by points.

The following are the points for Technical Skills only:

Score: 10 – knows everything, can do everything
         9 – excellent, can handle anything
         8 – very good, but needs practice
         7 – good, but needs more practice
         6 – sufficient, needs practice and training
         5 – can get by, needs more training
         4 – limited, needs training
         3 – can answer phone, needs lots of training
         2 – knows outline, but no details
         1 – has heard of it, seen it in action
         0 – nothing

Instructions

In Form A, scores are entered for technical skills and in Form B comments are entered for personal skills.

Note This is a very simple form and assessment method, and Figures 11.3 and 11.4 explain methods which are steps up from here and which produce a more balanced assessment result.

This is a simple assessment against the two matrices and does not take into account weighting of the technical or personal skills as they relate to the staff member's job or roles. An example would be 'Handling paper work': if the area only punched time cards as its paper work function, it could not carry the same assessed importance weighting as medical department staff taking information vital to operation and life-support decisions from forms in an intensive care unit.

The personal skills are evaluated in words by everyone to enable this part of the assessment to be more searching. The technical skills can be assessed through a written and/or practical test whereas personal skills are more difficult to gauge. However, recent advances such as the use of interactive videos and the like have established the means of testing personal skills too.

Another method of accomplishing the above assessment is for the AT to group the items in the Technical Skills Matrix into logical subsets (see Figure 11.3). These subsets could then be listed against each functional section of the department or area and points awarded as before; the weighting would then be easier. Personal skills would be handled as described in the first option in Figure 11.2.

Figure 11.3 Assessment form: more specific

Technical Skills	**Functional Section of the Department**			
	Office work	Welding shop	Assembly line	Etc.
Subsets				
Communication skills				
Performance under pressure				
Knowledge and use of manuals				
Computer capabilities	6	6	6	
Ability to see whole problem				
Knowledge and use of tools				
Disaster recovery ability				
Etc.				

The following are the points for Technical Skills only:

Score: 10 – knows everything, can do everything
         9 – excellent, can handle anything
         8 – very good, but needs practice
         7 – good, but needs more practice
         6 – sufficient, needs practice and training

5 – can get by, needs more training
4 – limited, needs training
3 – can answer phone, needs lots of training
2 – knows outline, but no details
1 – has heard of it, seen it in action
0 – nothing

Instructions The above form is specific to subsets of skills. It could be, and is, used for the personal skills assessment too.

Note A subset is a level above tasks, called functions, explained in Chapter 5. The functions are those which determined the list of tasks in the Technical Skills Matrix (shown in the Appendix to Chapter 7).

Along the top of the form are listed the areas in which the members of the department or work site are expected to work, called 'Functional Sections'. For example, the members are expected to carry out office work, work in the welding shop and on the assembly line. This allows the inclusion on the form of a maximum number of points to make the assessments better focused on the roles and functions of the members operating in this area. If the office was a minor part of the area's total work output, then the maximum points could be limited to two in most of the column entitled 'Office work', while the 'Welding shop' could have points up to eight or ten.

It is important for management to try each of these assessment forms themselves before actually using them on the people to be assessed. Even then, the first assessment should be a 'fun' assessment for both parts of the team to learn from so that the assessment system can be improved.

From Figure 11.3 it is clear the subsets can be applicable to many areas that may not seem to have any relationship to each other. 'Computer capabilities' is as valid a function in computerized welding equipment as it is in the office's use of personal computers. However, if the person is working mainly in the welding shop, the weighting factor may be seven times the score there whereas the score in the office has a weighting of only one (as shown in Figure 11.4). If the person scored six in both Office and Welding Shop, then the end weighted scores would be:

Office 6 x 1 = 6
Welding 6 x 7 = 42

This allows the resulting score to reflect the department's important roles and functions, and to reflect those with the biggest impact on the business plan and the customer.

Figure 11.4 Assessment form: more specific

	Functional Section of the Department			
Technical Skills	Office work	Welding shop	Assembly line	Etc.
Subsets	**Weighting Factors**			
Communication skills				
Performance under pressure				
Knowledge and use of manuals				
Computer capabilities	6 x 1 = 6	6 x 7 = 42	6 x 1 = 6	

(A reproducible blank form is provided as Appendix 1 at the end of this chapter.)

Final variation

In some areas it may be necessary to limit the number of points that can be awarded. In the example discussed earlier, if the office personal computer was operated to carry out only two tasks and the welding shop computer had many options and much scope, it might be that the maximum number of points possible would be four and ten respectively. This tied to the weighting gives a system of assessing all areas against the levels of ability required to carry out the function or task and the ability of the person being assessed, as shown in Figure 11.5. (A reproducible blank form is provided at the end of this chapter as Appendix 2.)

Figure 11.5 Assessment form: more specific
(weighted and point limits)

Technical Skills	Functional Section of the Department			
	Office work	Welding shop	Assembly line	Etc.
Subsets	**Points and Weighting Factors**			
Communication skills				
Performance under pressure				
Knowledge and use of manuals				
Computer capabilities	**4 - 1**	**10 - 7**	**8 - 7**	

Note: The **first number** in the square of each column is the maximum points available for that subset.

The **second number** is the weighting factor.

Note This is the best of the assessment forms. This format makes it easy to tailor the same form to the requirements of various departments in the same company. Each different department may wish to add or subtract some subsets or Functional Sections (see Note to Figure 11.3) but the areas of similarity will work from a standard base.

Figures 11.4 and 11.5 show instances where the points are varied and weighting factors are then added. The points are varied according to criteria determined by the company or department. As in Figure 11.3, office work may carry a maximum of two points in all areas for someone if office work has little impact on his or her daily work. But in this assessment form the points can be varied by subset and create a range for the whole department and company (as a standard).

The importance will vary from department to department, and to reflect this there is a weighting ability. We can take as an example 'Handling of Paper Work' from Figure 11.3. In area 1, which only punched time cards, the points on the form could be four, but the same four points would not be valid in area 2, the medical intensive care unit area. Weighting the two areas 1 and 10 respectively would help to balance the end result of the subset and assessments, with area 1 achieving four points multiplied by one weighting factor point, equalling four points, and area 2 achieving four points, multiplied by ten weighting factor points, which equals forty points.

The result of the scores and weighting factors now used would be:

Office 4 x 1 = 4
Welding 10 x 7 = 70

The system's ability to be altered to suit the needs of the

company and to be focused on the matrices is vital and is directly in line with people development. People are not being measured against production targets, quotas or the like but are being assessed on their abilities as a total person. The assessments indicate what training would be of value in the next six months.

A similar form and weighting system is used for the personal skills. As possessing good 'Team Leader' skills is harder than 'Punctuality', the weighting might be nine and two respectively.

Stage 2

After an agreed period (seven or fourteen days), the completed forms are returned to the Assessment Team by the people being assessed. The written and/or practical test(s) are determined, or driven, by these returned forms (see Figure 11.1). If the person says he or she knows nothing about computers, there is no need for the test to contain any questions on that subject. If the person indicates that he or she knows only about welding computers then all other questions or practical tests would contain only those areas.

What is this process achieves is *value testing*. The complete system detailed in this book is focused on changing all aspects of 'the way the company does business', including the assessment process.

If the AT determines that some of the subsets are not applicable to a section then that box on the form can be blacked out. The subsets will be compared to the Job Performance Guides (JPGs) which are clear guides for function and task accomplishment. The assessment forms are to be as user-friendly as possible, and the person being assessed must be able to discuss filling out the forms with Team Leaders.

Stage 3

Prior to the interview the AT will meet and compile a generic result on the forms described in Stage 1. This has proved to be one of the fairest systems, as the end result is a balanced assessment of both technical and personal skills.

The interview is also driven by the results of Stages 1 and 2. Time and effort are not wasted on areas already determined to be of no value, so effective interviews are now possible.

Using this system means that there are no surprises at any of the stages and the person being assessed is able to appraise himself or herself, knowing each stage will be driven by his or her own inputs.

The interview is a time when the AT can draw out further knowledge and experience which the person being assessed may have missed or overlooked. Also, any areas not correctly tested, in which the AT knows the person to have some ability, can be discussed and clarified.

Don't rush the interviews: four per day is fine. Start them early enough to be able to meet the completion date of every six months. The interviews are carried out on a *one-to-one basis*, using one assessment form compiled with the generic results from all AT members. If each member of the AT did four interviews per day and there were five on the AT, that equates to twenty per day. Give all staff ample notice of the interview dates and be willing to discuss the interview format and reasons for the format (i.e. helping people to develop).

Stage 4

Each person is issued with a letter giving the result of the assessment and an indication of the areas that need development during the next six months if that person is to advance to the next higher level. This is positive and enables the formal training and individual's self-learning to be directed only towards those areas needing time and effort. This is yet another value-adding part of the complete system.

(An example of this letter is shown in Appendix 3 at the end of this chapter.)

The results

The scoring of the technical and personal skills carries the most weight in this process. The important skills are those determined by the AT who have worked with the person under assessment.

The written and practical tests are to help determine the person's skills as measured against agreed standards (the JPGs). It is vital that the whole system is maintained and remains available to all staff. As the assessments are driven by the forms and ways of doing business everyone uses in the day-to-day operations of their department or area, it is only logical that they should be just a natural part of the way business is done.

The written or practical tests may be worth only 10 per cent of the total assessment figure. This will vary from company to company, and even from area to area within a company.

An example of a scoring system used is:

Areas Assessed		Worth
• Technical Skills Tests		8%
• Technical Skills Assessed		46%
• Personal Skills Assessed		46%
	Total	100%

It is important to keep the Personal Skills as a high percentage of the total because the development of the whole person is vital.

The system is simple and can be used easily at department or area level.

Salaries

There is a need for the matrices of the various functions within the company to be measured and for salaries to be established fairly. This would normally be an executive (corporate) responsibility, but in this system it is done by a team made up of members from the different areas within the company. Their role is to create the levels of functions and related salaries.

It is important to remember that anyone in the company can upset or drive away customers if he or she is not part of the overall team environment. This system eliminates much of the need for salaries to be higher in one area than another just because it has always been that way or because the job title dictated it.

If the company pays top of the barrel salaries, it will get top of the barrel people. If the right people are in the right jobs in the right numbers, offering the company better skills and hence better value, it will be a whole lot easier to pay top of the barrel salaries. There will be a strong company base to support it, and the strength will have been created by these same 'right' people.

The CEO must be the first to start the process by determining how many of the people directly reporting to him or her are the right people. 'Proof of the need' can be applied here: How many are the right people and how many are there for all the wrong reasons? If $US2 billion companies can be operated with a head office of just fifteen people, how many people do you need? Not many questions need to be asked before the answer is established. Ask 'why' a number of times and the real answer will be found:

Why does that function exist?
(Answer)
Why?
(Answer)
Why?
(And so on)

If it is proved that the function is needed, then ask where else the function could be carried out so that it is responsive, value adding, reliable, timely, customer-focused and so on.

This same logic must be used in a cascading effect throughout the company. It should take weeks rather than months for the restructuring to be completed and the training to commence in earnest at all levels.

It is hard only if management make it hard. Make the decision! Then just 'do it'!

It is so much fun to be part of this new process, and everyone who is the right person in the right job will want to come to work every day. It is a simple Do-It-Yourself process and the resultant system is habitual and continuous.

Team Leaders

As discussed, Team Leaders are necessary, and their role can be either paid or unpaid. However, if payment is made, it will be harder to rotate people through the leadership role. The aim of the system is for everyone to become a self-leader and hence reduce the amount of supervision throughout the company. If attention is drawn to the payment or part-payment for part of a month as Team Leader, then attention is taken away from the function.

It must remain clear that being Team Leader, as part of the training, is part of the *development of the person* and enables that team member to be better able to contribute to the team.

This is not a drive to eliminate all supervision but rather to identify those supervisors and the like who are not required (because each team member becomes better able to make value decisions through the other team members). The supervisors could perhaps be better used in research and development or in following up on the flood of ideas generated by the new successfully implemented company environment.

Team member roles

Team members in this new environment will be required to carry out the hiring of new staff. They will call and chair production, weekly, performance, customer-focus and other types of meetings. New ideas will have to be discussed with peers, team leaders and management in order to arrive at the best solution.

These discussions are not held to get a signature, a 'nod' or any other authorization required under the old systems, but are to solicit ideas and suggestions that can be added to the final decision and solution. As the majority of the work can be found at the front line, shouldn't a proportionate amount of decision making take place there too?

These functions and tasks become part of the normal day, and whether or not they are paid for individually will be up to each company. It has been proved, through successful implementations, that the ability of staff to affect the way the business is run outweighs the requirement for salary payments. Other rewards are needed; a reward system is discussed in Chapter 14.

Appendix 1

Assessment form: more specific

	Functional Section of the Department			
Technical Skills				
Subsets				

Appendix 2

Figure 11.4 Assessment form: more specific

	Functional Section of the Department			
Technical Skills				
Subsets	**Points and Weighting Factors**			

Appendix 3

Assessment Result Letter

Confidential

To   :
From   : The Assessment Team
Date   :
Subject : Assessment result

Following the assessments completed during the previous six weeks the Assessment Team has determined the following:

You have been assessed at level:

You demonstrated levels of Technical Skills and Personal Skills consistent with the next level except for the following:

Technical Skills	Personal Skills
_____	_____
_____	_____
_____	_____

Some formal training will be scheduled for you during the next six months and will mainly target Personal Skills, but you are reminded of the need to self-learn technical skills.

You are congratulated on your fine efforts and achievements and the excellent result you have achieved.

Please plan ahead now with your Team Leader to enable you to achieve another excellent result at the next assessment, on   /   /19 .

Signature

12

Training

Training is still viewed by many companies as a cost, and when the going gets tough the training budget gets the going over. Training must be considered as an extremely vital part of any company's targets and goals. If companies are not constantly training their people to keep them updated, motivated, and improved, the competition may end up with all of their good people. This will leave the original companies scraping a living or worse.

Most companies have individuals who, although they are very good technically, no one likes to be around because of their personalities. Then there are those who are really great people but cannot carry out even the simplest of the technical tasks required of them. There is also a third group who have reached a plateau and for whom the road ahead is indistinct or non-existent, so they have no motivation to do more. All three of these groups contribute to the problems faced by companies today.

However, there is a fourth group: those all-rounders who have achieved a balance between technical and personal skills.

The investment in training is sometimes quite hard to justify when looked at as a simple equation involving the returns made. How much the company earned, saved or lost as a result of one or one thousand hours of training is often anyone's guess.[1] An example of one company's belief in training was the reply given by Federal Express (of Memphis, Tennessee, USA) when asked the cost per year per employee of training: 'We do not know, all

---

1. This is 'The 1000% Factor', a term coined by Jan Carlzon, President, Scandinavian Air System (SAS), Stockholm, Sweden.

we know is the great results we have achieved because of the training.'

So we know training is of value, though unquantifiable monetarily, but how does a company ensure that the training is both targeted and value-adding?

There are many kinds of training and a quick look through the Yellow Pages and newspapers demonstrates this. The training our team considered was the training required for people to:

1. develop through the matrices
2. be effective team members.

These were the two most important aspects, and the department (and company) had also adopted the Total Quality Management Concept, which the Matrix Concept supports perfectly. Indeed that is why it was developed: the old systems did not and could not work effectively in the new TQM environment.

The team now understood that the Matrix Concept was constructed to enable the company to achieve its goals through its people, and the team did not lose sight of the fact that staff improvement in (1) and (2) above would lead directly to the company's objectives.

Types of training

Three types of training were evident from the Matrix Concept:

1. Technical skills.
2. Business skills.
3. Personal skills.

Technical skills are those skills related to the accomplishment of the functions and tasks required to carry out the day-to-day operations of the department *effectively*.

Business skills are those skills required to improve the *efficiency* of the operations, to determine and analyse these improvements, and arrive at innovative solutions.

Personal skills are those *personal characteristics and virtues* required of people to enable them to be effective team members and team leaders, balanced against their right and ability to be an individual.

The Matrix Concept is aimed at developing the complete person. The team decided that the best way to develop a training programme was to view the methods available for the three training types (see Figure 12.1).

Figure 12.1 Methods of accomplishing training

Type	Internal	External
Technical Skills	• On-Job-Training • Internal trainers	• Outside trainers* • Outside schools
Business Skills	• In-house courses • TQM in-house • Internal trainers • Management coaching	• Outside courses • Outside trainers
Personal Skills	• internal trainers • On-Job-training • Management coaching	• Outside courses • Outside trainers
* Outside trainers would come into the company.		

It is important for the management to be part of the training process wherever possible. The profile of management has to change radically from the old dictatorial style to a coaching role. This is explained in Chapter 13.

The key is for management to be skilled first in the new methods and then train the company's people. This enables both the management and the front-line workforce to:

- work to common goals
- work to common business practices
- use a common language in the company
- have similar training
- have single-source training where possible.

The need for management to be more involved and for the training to be value-adding puts a completely different profile on training. No longer would it be correct for staff members X, Y and Z to be sent on any course that popped up in the mail, just to meet the training hours' target, as is often the case currently:

> (Manager shouts across the office or plant) 'Hey Joe, you are going on the Sales Training course next week.'
> (Joe replies) 'I don't need it.' or 'I did that last month.'
> (The manager shouts back) 'That's OK, you are the only one I can spare and I'll be able meet my target for Training Hours Achieved.'

The team wanted the new empowerment and team environment to work. It was now necessary to explain why the training was being carried out and why staff were selected to attend. This environment cannot be achieved only partially, rather it is an all-or-nothing environment. To accomplish the training determined (Figure 12.1) the team decided that the overriding criterion was: As much as possible of the training of the staff would be Do-It-Yourself. That is, the company itself would carry out as much of the training as possible to encourage ownership of the problems and the results. This was dependent on the company demonstrating its ability to remain up to date with the new demands of the new environment.

The following course of action was adopted:

1. *Technical skills*:

On-Job-Training by co-workers would deliver the best results. The technical skills were those actions and abilities determined by the staff through the matrix system. These skills were best known by the experts — the company's own staff doing the job today. Visits to other companies were commenced to see what other techniques were available and in use.

Also, staff were allowed to have discussions with agencies about new products and services which might improve the way the company carried out the processes. This was after the initial improvements to the processes had been made.

2. *Business skills*:

We had a Total Quality Management trainer in house and the TQM process includes the teaching of business skills. The ability to look at processes well 'outside of the square' was encouraged by management, as was directed risk-taking.

Certain skills, such as financial training, project management, and time management, required external training.

Where possible the training was acquired by management and then taught by them to the staff. There are very few quicker ways of learning something than by trying to train someone else effectively.

3. *Personal skills*:

External training was used quite extensively here. There are many training companies which offer off-the-shelf packages in this often rather delicate area. The team decided that off-the-shelf courses were fine for the past but not for today and certainly not for the future.

Many outside companies offered 'supervisory' courses and would not be shaken from those. Those companies were not selected as they clearly demonstrated they were not listening to the customer (our team). 'Off the shelf' means that the course is tailored to the average company or average needs. We were no longer an average company and no longer had average needs.

Single sourcing proved excellent as the training group grew along with the department. Because the external training group was with us, there was no longer a need for our team to constantly explain the radical changes occurring. When management were trained or the staff were retrained that training reflected an understanding of our problems and successes never before experienced with external trainers. The external trainers were neither pushy nor laid back but were there at the right time with the right product and service.

Innovative training has to be worked at. There are no short cuts, and both the company and the external trainers have to contribute. The external trainers must be constantly challenging their products and services and methods. Our team's training methods included the use of actresses, opera singers and other high profile guest speakers, 'hi-jacking' the attendees and sailing.

Many of the staff felt that this was another flavour-of-the-month effort from management, and that if they could just hang in there it would all pass by as these new ideas had always done in the past. But it finally began to dawn on everyone that this time the 'system' was driving the whole process and that it was here to stay, because:

- the department's layout changed physically so that there were no internal walls or manager's office
- the single job title was firmly in place
- the training was in line with the new environment
- their peers began to criticize them for not contributing
- no one was listening to tales of how great it all was before.

If it is left to the drive of one person, the process is doomed to failure. We have been studying a system that makes the whole process habitual and institutionalized. There must be inspired leadership, and effort not from just one but from as many people as can be brought on board.

Bringing people on board was easy. The new system could deliver what the management and staff members wanted in their workplace, notably:

- to have career development paths
- to know what is expected of a person at work
- to be able to try out all their ideas
- to train others and be trained in order to develop
- to have pay/salary levels tied to technical and personal skills developed.

A well-managed matrix system's ability to meet and exceed the people's expectations makes it hard to turn down. The unions also found the same process too tempting to resist and came on board. And why not? There is no blame/shame or us/them in this system. It is a system that will continue when staff join, change or leave for any reason — it is a system that works.

As the system can exceed many of the customers' (the company's members') expectations, it is only natural and to their advantage for them to commit themselves wholeheartedly to make it work.

Knowing what and when to train

Technical skills

The matrices created for the department clearly provided the technical skills and allowed determination of the personal aptitudes needed to accomplish them, along with the personal skills required by the department's new team structure.

Internally, On-Job-Training was used to promote the multi-skilling of the staff. The dramatic staff reductions that occurred over a period of one day created an impetus for the remaining staff to gain this multi-skilling as soon as possible.

Management in the area had sometimes to fill in for the

shortages created during the first thirty to ninety days. Staff were placed in areas with which they had some previous familiarity and where they could develop to an acceptable level in a reasonably short period of time.

New staff had been recruited into the department and they could see the opportunity for development offered by Matrix Concept, and so put extra effort into developing multi-skills. Their efforts sparked off extra training by those who were comfortable in the roles they had had prior to the establishment of the Matrix Concept. The long-term staff had not previously faced this threat of other staff being able to exceed them in skill. In the old job-title environment other staff were shown only the little they needed, because information was power. Now the environment was one which required everyone in the 'team' to be trained and to develop multi-skills in many areas.

No longer could anyone hold back information or knowledge. Peer pressure opened all doors and staff felt a sense of development and growth that brought enjoyment and fun to the workplace.

Technical skill development was the main focus for the first two to four months for all staff. Even those who thought they were the experts found the need to teach and learn invigorating.

Personal skills

Development of the people side of the staff was as important as the enhancement of technical skills. The handling of most management advancement is summed up by what one manager said some time ago: 'I was put into this job as manager without any training and I turned out OK, so why should I train any of the up-and-coming staff? If it was good enough for me, then it should be good enough for them.'

The fact that he assessed himself as OK was the first problem because he was assessed as 'needs to be replaced' by his company, and indeed he was replaced. The fact that he was not trained is not an excuse for failing to train everyone else. If he had fallen down the stairs at work, would that have meant that he had to throw all his staff down the stairs, just because it had happened to him? His 'fear' was that the up-and-coming staff would overtake him in ability and that the company would find him to be expendable. That was his comment after he was eventually replaced.

It was not his fault alone. The company should have developed him as a complete person instead of just advancing him because his technical skills were very good.

Our team decided that the skills had to be broader than just the technical skills and should include presentation skills, counselling skills and similar abilities to be developed in all the staff. To achieve this a questionnaire was created and distributed to all staff to gain information on weak areas among individuals and within the team. (This is shown in Appendix 1 at the end of this chapter. The form shown in the Appendix is a shortened version of that actually used. The areas for training would normally number sixty or more and would cover aspects common to business in general and those unique to a particular company.)

The results compiled from the combined responses gave the first indication of the skills, other than technical, that needed to be developed and of the training that had to be designed and scheduled.

The management team had also determined their own list of ten skills, and when this was compared to the results from the survey, there was only one difference. This was an excellent indication to the management team of the fact that the people really did want to develop and that they had a very good understanding and grasp of the business.

The resultant training was, in the main, actually designed by the people themselves. It can be seen why off-the-shelf training from internal or external training groups would no longer be acceptable: the needs of different teams would be different and so the training had to be tailored to suit.

The Personal Skills Matrix contained the personal

development needs necessary to fit into the new team environment. This made the development of training much easier for our team and the training groups we dealt with, or it should have.

Over one dozen external training groups and the company's own training group were requested to bid for the ongoing training of the people in the new environment. Each company was given a presentation lasting an hour or more on the changes our department had just gone through and what was expected from the training. All of the groups commented on how radical the changes were and said that they had not seen anything like these changes before. Even so, some of the companies offered 'supervisor' training when we stated we no longer had supervisors. Some offered off-the-shelf packages when they had already been told this was not an option we would consider. A couple actually listened to us and offered training that was startling, innovative, memorable and enjoyable and (most importantly) tailored to our unique needs. Much of the training was actually cheaper than off-the-shelf generic packages.

The staff enjoyed the training and the most frequent comment expressed how valuable and in line with our needs the training was. So it should be — after all, they designed it themselves for the most part. All the management had to do was work with the training company to organise the training, venues, aids, and so on.

Are you wondering about the response from the company training department? They claimed that if training was not off the shelf, they did not want to know about it — it was too hard and offered no real return to their area. Sound familiar?

This form of training has to be ongoing. The company cannot expect new ideas and results if there is no training to spur on the flow of ideas and directed risk-taking. Training encourages and helps bind the team members together and confirms the need for fringe thinkers: those who think outside the square regularly. Maybe this tendency will rub off as the risks and results (both good and bad) are celebrated.

Celebrating good results is common, but is not done very frequently in most companies. Celebrating failures that were in line with the missions, goals and effort of the company is not only uncommon, but the failures are usually hidden. Take a step outside what is accepted as normal, and the pent-up potential released by this form of celebrating, when people see it is OK to fail sometimes, will stagger you.

Business skills and project teams

Training in business skills formed part of the Total Quality Management training course held by the in-house instructor. This is excellent training because it questions every aspect of business and accepted 'ways of doing business around here'.

Following this training, and while all the changes were taking place, projects were commenced. This was important because staff were told about empowerment and they had to experience it as soon as possible. Within the first week of the changes the first Project Team was formed.

A new layout for the area made it clear to everyone that the change was permanent, and the layout was designed by the people themselves. The need for a new layout was clear from the process of JPG development: it was determined that a better layout would promote easier ways to do work and shorten processes.

Volunteers were sought for the Project Team and they carried out the project in line with a project letter constructed by management (see Figure 12.2). This was an important type of training and an important stage in people development. This form of project work produced multiple benefits:

- it provided training in project management
- it clearly demonstrated management's commitment
- it was the first empowerment exercise and test
- it allowed staff to apply the business skills learned
- it made application of TQM mandatory

- it kept staff focused on the new direction and efforts required in the environment
- it was an additional step in team building
- it was the training ground for participation in bigger projects.

Figure 12.2 Project letter

Project 1: **Office Layout** Date: 12/12/19 .

Objective
To review and improve the current department layout and complete all changes that will benefit and encourage the new 'team' environment, multi-skilling and work practices.

Considerations
1. Team building is vital
2. The new environment requires a layout that will:
    - promote good communications
    - improve customer services
    - improve the quality of work
    - enable cross training
    - promote multi-skilling
3. Lighting/windows/air/safety etc. to be incorporated

Expectations
- All staff in the area will be surveyed
- The Project Team works to consensus decisions
- The new layout will be process and function effective and efficient

Requirements
1. The Project Team will use the next seven days to select a Team Leader and determine the amount and type of work involved to complete the study.

---

2. On the eighth day the project Leader will discuss the total project completion plan and milestone chart with management.

3. The Project Team will carry out the project in accordance with the agreed plan and milestone chart.

4. Management to be kept informed at agreed points.

Team Members
The following are the volunteers for this project, and it is to be completed on a no-overtime basis as agreed.
Name 1, Name 2, Name 3, Name 4, Name 5

(A blank letter is provided in Appendix 2 at the end of this chapter.)

This first project was not completed on time, but that was not the point. The people on the project team were learning their new roles, as were the management. To take on a project or to change something required new skills. No longer was it acceptable to bitch and complain. The new 'way of doing business' was simple: if you have any ideas at all, put them forward, but not to management. Put the ideas to your peers and together work through the definition of the improvement or idea, the analysis, the ideas to improve the defined areas, how the implementation will be carried out, and how the whole package will be sold to everyone concerned.

There was now no room in the department for anyone to complain about anything. The new way of doing business was for solutions to be found by the people. What a great way to run a business, so that every idea you ever had could be considered and, if accepted by your peers and management as appropriate and in line with the direction of the company, implemented.

How do you sell the idea to peers and management? Get them involved in the project as team members. They cannot say no if they are on the team that came up with the solution.

Ongoing training

The training never stops. If it does, every aspect of the business will suffer. The answer is not to have more and more machinery but to enable the people to improve the whole process. How many people get up in the morning to do a bad day's work? If the answer is none, then why do companies appear to treat people as if they did?

People will see the opportunities to shorten or eliminate processes, to reduce or eliminate waste (inventory, work in progress, motion, over-processing, rework, etc.), be innovative and customer-aware, be responsive to and listen to the customer, and accomplish so many, many more things. But to achieve this there must be targeted training, and when it is completed, more must be scheduled.

Responsibility

There are two areas of training responsibility: management's (or the company's) and the people's responsibility. The end result of both responsibilities is to achieve continuous training of all staff — not daily but regularly and consistently. The Matrix Concept makes this requirement part of the system.

With each staff member having a personal copy of the matrices and each member being evaluated regularly during the year there is a constant demand for training and improvement. Management's role is to schedule some time during normal working hours when people will be trained for a day, a week and so on. This is also part of the company's demonstration of its commitment to its members.

Individuals will self-learn during their days off, when not on shift, or when there are quiet times during the work day. The personal matrices will guide the individual and target the training. This way the staff member is carrying out only value-adding training, and management can support and guide this.

Teamwork will result as one individual trains another at the correct times. Much of the training will be arranged between team members without any action from management.

The old style of management was simple: everyone should be busy all the time they are at work (which usually was not the case). The manager used to come out of the office and survey all he or she 'owned' and if everyone was doing something then that was OK, but if not then look out for the stick!

If there is no work, the people are simply producing costs. There are times in all systems when there may not be any work to be carried out, so the staff member should not produce costs but rather invest that available time in some form of training that adds value. The speed of learning is now very much up to the individuals, and management is there to coach and encourage at appropriate rates.

Training standards are also created by the staff and management together, and used as additional support in the regular coaching, training, and assessments.

Low cost/no cost results

The majority of improvements during the first two years are low cost or no cost. The opportunities are mainly the reduction or elimination of processes or parts of processes which the company is already carrying out. Usually only in a few cases is there a need to spend very large sums of money. It is not technology that will give the company its cash flows and margins, but the company's *ability to do the 'right things right, first time'*.

Summary

The costs of training have always been in the minds of those in charge of the purse strings of a company. When the company experiences hard times one of the first areas to be hit is the training budget, if there is one. This is because of the way training has been carried out in the past. The training was not targeted and was sometimes only vaguely value-adding, if at all.

This attitude among the purse-string holders was caused by the old way of meeting training-hour quotas and not being able to show the real value of training. After all, they had to meet the same quotas.

The two matrices developed through the Matrix Concept give detailed training needs both for individuals and for the teams.

Total Quality Management and the Matrix Concept are exactly matched and directed towards achieving the same results of:

- people development and empowerment to enable them to capture customers through quality, reliability, consistency, and price
- making the company stronger
- maintaining and providing jobs.

Multi-skilling and business skill development enable all people to make better decisions. The goal of every company must be to remove the blinkered attitude of 'my desk, my phone, my job' and grant all staff the ability to know the impact of decisions on the broader and bigger picture.

The Matrix Concept makes this demand habitual as part of the system and does not leave it to any one person or group.

We had now:
10. determined training would be ongoing, and determined the types, responsibilities and impacts of training

---

Appendix 1

Training and Skills Questionnaire

Please complete the following questions and return this form to
_____ by (date) _____.

Name: Date:

Part A

Please indicate if you have ever had any training in any of the
following areas, and indicate the approximate year of the
training.*

Communications

1. Writing reports
2. Writing formal letters
3. Making presentations
4. Listening skills
5. Telephone conversations
6. Giving verbal instructions
7. Training others
8. Verbal comms over radios

Business

9. Cost controls
10. Decision making
11. Problem solving
12. Goal setting
13. Team membership
14. Training others
15. Motivation
16. Planning
17. Quality
18. Leadership
19. Delegation
20. Team work

Customer Service

21. Keeping cool
22. How to be nice
23. How to serve
24. Service delivery

Part B

From the list above list the ten areas that you feel will be most valuable in your role within the department. If there are some not listed above please enter them here (Maximum of ten).

Order

1. _____ ___
2. _____ ___
3. _____ ___
4. _____ ___
5. _____ ___
6. _____ ___
7. _____ ___
8. _____ ___
9. _____ ___
10. _____ ___

Part C

In the list above, please rate them as the most imprtant (1) to the least important (10) in the column 'Order'.

* The lists in Part A would normally be sixty or more items long to cover all areas applicable to the department or area, including: communications, business, customer service, production, manufacturing, service, etc.

The topics in this form could be increased to allow about ten to twelve words under each topic heading to explain what the topic means with regard to training content, so those completing it would be better informed.

As an example, for item 1 on the above form under the heading 'Communications', the topic would be expanded:

(1)Writing reports

- collecting, grouping, sifting information
- when/when not to write
- writing winning reports
- etc.

When the forms are returned the answers would be evaluated to indicate:

From Part A of the form:

The overall ability of the department as a team in the various areas being assessed. If Topics 1 to 24 (in our sample form above) were also shown as (1) experienced, (2) limited and (3) none, then each member could tick one of these as to their view of their ability in each area. The result would give an additional dimension to the results.

From Part B of the form:

The critical items for training as perceived by the customer of the training: our team member. Management will have certain knowledge and expectations too, but this question enables a balance to be achieved between what the team member personally wants and what is required of the whole team for the betterment of the overall skills and capabilities of all members. The whole department, the company and especially the customer will gain when these results are translated into rigorous training programmes.

From Part C of the form:

The *order* gives the importance rating across the board too. For building the training, Part B is vital. It will make less and less *off-the-shelf* training acceptable. Training coordinators will have to source training groups who will tailor training courses at the right price.

Appendix 2

Project Letter

Project:	Date: / /19

Objective

Considerations
1.

Expectations

Requirements
1.

2.

Team Members
The following are the volunteers for this project, and it is to be completed on a no-overtime basis as agreed.

The project letter forms the basis of the briefing with the team, and is not meant to replace that important aspect of communicating the desired objectives (see Figure 12.2). It does help both management and the Project Team to understand the deliverables.

Instructions

1. *Project title*
Should be simple and indicate the main project focus.

2. *Objective*
Should give clear indication of the scope, actions required (review and implementation, etc.) and purpose of the project.

3. *Considerations*
Should list those main factors of interest that would be the minimum to be investigated and analysed before the project could be completed.

4. *Expectations*
Should state those factors which impact on the process by which the project is carried out.

5. *Requirements*
Should express the mandatory parts of the project, such as reporting dates, the need for a team leader, how reporting will be carried out and between whom, etc. It would also include indications of how project work times and completion dates are to be determined.

6. *Team Members*
Should show those team members who have either volunteered or were selected for the project, with their contact phone numbers, addresses, etc. This makes it easy for anyone with input or interest to have access to the Project Team.

Project letters should be distributed so everyone knows that the project is in progress. This process eliminates duplication of efforts or resources.

13

The new role of management

Without doubt, in the whole of the process discussed in this book, the notion of a new role for management was one of the hardest concepts to sell and implement. Management have always known they are right, simply by virtue of being management. The belief that 'I am the boss and therefore I am right' has created an atmosphere in which people are no longer

willing to challenge, and this falsely endorses management's belief. As stated in Chapters 1 and 2, management have created the companies as they are today—no one else could have done so!

In the past, management quite rightly made decisions based on what they knew. To say one did not know something was a clear sign of weakness, or so it was thought. Changing one's mind fitted into the same category of weakness. There were a few pioneers, but the 'old system' would eventually bring them into line, making the atmosphere so bad that they would eventually leave; or these rockers of boats would be given tasks of a value equal to counting wind surfers in Antarctica.

Management were perceived to be the only decision makers and the company environment reflected that. If the customers wanted something just outside the rules, they were requested to wait while the front-line staff member went to ask the supervisor (at whatever level), who may then have had to ask someone on the next layer of supervision, and so on up the ladder. By the time the answer came back down the customers were gone and had taken everyone they knew with them.

The important point is that, because of the way the company structure worked, customer satisfaction or dissatisfaction would be reported in the monthly report and a meeting would be called a month later to discuss it. This environment of rigid, slow-moving structures with poor communication and unquestioning staff is the environment towards which implementation of the Matrix Concept must be directed.

Management created today's companies and, quite rightly, only management can fundamentally change them; but change to what?

There is a common theme in the startling successes of many companies around the world. They all empowered and enabled the people in the company to be and do better. Management must consider how to accomplish this change in a structured and logical way. Adopting the Matrix Concept directly supports the transition to and continuance of the environment of empowerment and enablement that is a fundamental feature of these successful companies.

The task of management is easier when it is determined by the status quo. Most decisions that need to be made have probably been made once or more already. Most management are comfortable in this nearly risk-free environment. Work can be directed without the need to explain what or why, and sitting in offices writing memos, drinking coffee and enjoying the get-togethers with other management staff under the guise of meetings is regarded as a normal day's work. Maintenance of a status quo invented by management has put companies and countries where they are today.

The new environment for management

The results of the past management practices are clear to everyone who listens to the radio, watches television or reads newspapers and magazines. The majority of stories are not good and the future is even worse for companies which stay within the status quo.

The new management environment is one in which the workforce and front-line people are trained, empowered, and enabled to do more as teams. This demands a management style that complements the team.

Management must let go of the attitude that only they can make worthwhile decisions regarding business, customers, spending money, and the like. Many staff will not be able to make this transition overnight or even in the early months of reconstructuring. Indeed, many staff do not really know what is expected of them in their daily work today, but this is management's responsibility.

Did you get up this morning and say to yourself 'I must get to work to read the company's Policies and Procedures Manual'? Probably not, and yet that is where many directives from management end up. The staff doing the actual work, at any level, know best how to improve it, so let them.

A demonstration of the fact that the use of a lot of words leads to the use of even more words and that clarity diminishes in direct proportion to the increase in the number of words, is provided by Figure 13.1.

Figure 13.1 Interesting numbers

Topic	Number of words
The Lord's Prayer	56
The Ten Commandments	73
Lincoln's Gettysburg Address	266
USA Price Control Commission Order on Cabbage prices	26 000

Are long and wordy policies and procedures the answer, or is it the spirit and understanding of the people that is really important? Taking these same people and offering them the ability to make decisions, is exciting and it is very satisfying to watch the development of all the company's people. Getting down to the simplest level, the management of today and tomorrow must love to see people growing in ability and achieving success after success.

The following *is* the new environment for management.

1. **Team Member**
A major role in the new management environment is that of being seen as a team member, as demonstrated by:

- Being more in the workplace than in the office.
- Setting time aside to sit in on team meetings (wherever they are) as a team member and not necessarily as the leader. Let the staff select the leader. Maybe it will be you, but you could contribute more simply through membership of the team.

- Contributing time, effort and ideas in support of the team and maintaining your responsibilities and actions as the team progresses.

2. **Leading**

A second major role is that of getting the team involved in goal and target setting, where the goals and targets are not quotas but levels of quality, reliability and consistency in service and products delivered to both the internal and external customers. This involves:

- *Measuring and achieving agreed targets, such as: amounts of waste eliminated, innovations implemented, process improvements made, and so on.*

- Ensuring adequate resources are available to the team, including time, funds, training, advice, specialists, facilities, and also trips which assist the development of the staff, processes, products and services delivered to the customers and the company as a whole.

Most of the leadership is by consensus, but, in the few instances when this is not possible, lead from the front, and if the environment is right members will follow wholeheartedly.

3. **Coaching**

This means:

- Enjoying the team's activity and *ensuring their efforts are directed towards agreed targets and goals*, which are in line with the company's missions and goals.

- Taking time to listen to the team members' problems, ideas, opinions, desires, and expectations.

- Making sure that staff understand that they have the opportunity to decide how best to achieve cost-effective customer satisfaction and then get on with the job, with you as team member and coach.

4. **Cheerleader**
- Encouraging team members, whoever they are, to achieve the agreed goals through celebrations both small and not so small but befitting genuine efforts and results.

5. **Communicator**
- Maintaining effective and efficient communication with team members, so that the customers are also viewed as team members.

- *Creating democratic communication, where there is true freedom of speech* within the company, so that everyone feels they can express their views and that these views are important enough to be listened to. Management must also encourage peers to work out ideas and problems together and bring problems and solutions to others, thereby eliminating the need to complain and enabling everyone to act on problems.

- Acknowledging that there is a much greater opportunity to meet and exceed company goals and customer expectations when everyone feels they have the right and obligation to change things which impinge negatively on both these areas.

6. **Trainer**
- Training, evaluating, assisting and advising in areas for development within the scopes defined, and make additional resources available where necessary.

- *Taking the time to do this well.*

7. **Customer retention**
- Ensuring that everyone is 'customer-sensitive' to be able to target and retain every customer the company can profitably

maintain. Retaining 5 per cent of existing customers can improve profits by up to 100 per cent.[1]

Focusing on customer retention drives everyone towards elimination of wasteful practices; there just is not time for these any more. This driver also gives a clear indication from management as to those processes and risks that are acceptable and those that are not.

8. **Manage**

There is very little time to be sitting behind the nice desk, in the nice office, drinking the nice cup of coffee, writing the nice memos in this environment.

- Expect the rate of change to accelerate in this new environment. The change will be focused, consistent and intensely experienced. *This is where competitive advantage occurs: in a people environment which is driven by all company members; where technology, instructions, policies, procedures and money become the tools of the people, rather than being resented for restricting and hampering progress and innovations.*

- Manage the continual transformation process, through your team of focused staff members to meet (and exceed if viable) the customers' expectations, *by constantly improving 'the way the company does business' ... through its people.*

The new management environment is one in which the people (front-line and workforce) are not 'controlled' by supervisors in a ratio of one to ten. These people are em-powered to make decisions with less and less supervision. The same effect occurs

---

1. F. F. Reichheld and W. E. Sasser Jr, 'Zero defections', *Harvard Business Review.* (1991) Sept/Oct.

throughout all levels of the company, and this creates a flatter structure.

I can think of no great teams that have achieved excellent results without a good, trustful, all round coach/leader; and this is *management's new role*. New role? It has always been their role, only it was ignored by so many in the past.

In some companies today, empowering the company's workforce means they do the hiring and firing, they hold production and staff meetings, they are able to spend money, change policies and procedures. It means time clocks are often eliminated and job titles are not important whereas what you can contribute to the team is. This simply means that all the people in the company are working for the same goals and targets (see Figure 13.2).

An environment in which the goals and targets are agreed upon by consensus, each area's contribution to the final result is known, and efforts are made to achieve the results eliminates the need and ability to have territory, or 'us and them' and 'my desk, my phone, my job' attitudes.

Management must motivate staff as team members, and must understand that, although they may believe they know what motivates people, they may be very much off the mark. That we do not always know what motivates people, whoever they are, even with preconditioning, is illustrated by the following story.

A very rich Texan had a daughter who had just reached marrying age, so he decided to hold a Coming Out party. He invited to his ranch all the eligible bachelors from within a radius of twenty-five miles. At the party, when the clock struck midnight the Texan led all these young men out to the swimming pool which he had filled with alligators and poisonous snakes. He then said he would give the first man who swam the full length of the pool one of these three prizes: 2000 acres of his prime land, $2 million cash, or his daughter's hand in marriage and, in time, all he owned.

He had no sooner finished speaking than there was a loud splash at one end of the pool and almost instantly a dripping wet young man got out at the other end. Now the Texan thought he knew what had motivated the young man, but when questioned the young man said he did not want any of the prizes.

The Texan was amazed so he asked, 'Well, what do you want?' And the young man replied, 'I want to know the name of that dude who pushed me into the swimming pool!'

Figure 13.2 Understanding all contributions

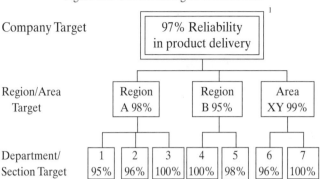

1. This is the point at which the reward for performance is determined for all staff in the company. It is simply a case of everyone gets something or everyone gets nothing. To give one department or person this kind of reward and give nothing to others is a sure way to destroy any team.

This type of chart could be made for production, service delivery, quality, marketing, operations, and finance.

All parts of the company know what they contribute, and, to improve their contribution, each part must work with other parts. There are no rewards at any level except at the *company* level, so there are no bonus points issued for one area doing well while another does badly, as it is the *final* company target achievement that brings rewards.

Here directed risk taking is encouraged and mistakes become accepted so that all members of staff may learn from them and build on the results, knowledge and experiences freely communicated. This is *not* pie in the sky but is actually happening in companies today.

14

Reward systems

The concept of 'reward' is most often confused with pay and salary. Because of this confusion companies have strikes, too many meetings and an us-and-them environment. The individual must be 'rewarded' for individual growth and worth, and there must be a separate 'reward' for performance of the team.

Reward is an award for achievements that can be related to efforts and productivity. Rewards are best issued as the result of team performance.

Salary/pay is the payment made in recognition of an individual's position and personal development in both technical and personal skills.

There is clearly a difference. The company's system must achieve a balance between the individual's needs and those of the team. This would not be achieved if the two were combined in one payment.

If an individual has individual targets which require no, or very limited, support from the team, the team will break up. There are many programmes in industry today that have names relating to teams but which in fact accomplish exactly the opposite of team building. However, it is clear that the individual is very important — the Matrix Concept is focused on the individual and his or her constant development.

This development is directly in line with what the company wants too, but there is deliberately no mention of time to do the job (in the JPGs, Chapter 10) and there are no production targets set there either. This is because that part of the system is the individual's part. Now we must look at the team and company performance.

Team reward — through performance

To measure performance and for that measurement to have meaning first requires that there be a target. The target is best agreed by the team members, but of which teams? The best situation is for the *company team* reach agreement and then establish support for each other, as shown in the last chapter in Figure 13.2 (reproduced below as Figure 14.1).

Once this agreement is in place there will be no room for an 'us and them' attitude; instead there must be mutual support to achieve the goals and the rewards common to all company members.

Figure 14.1 (from 13.1) Understanding all contributions

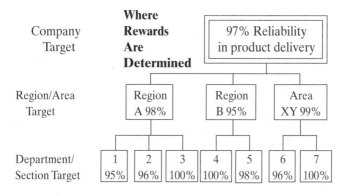

The system must establish rewards for the performance of the company. Each department or area's performance is a contributing factor, but the company as a whole must operate as a team to please the customer, eliminate waste, improve ROI and so on.

This part of the system establishes rewards, not salaries. We established salaries in Chapter 11.

The reward system must be meaningful to everyone at whatever level within the company, matrix and so on. One way to do this is to give everyone a salary-related reward only if the company makes a profit. That would be, say, once a year and should be up to a maximum of four months' salary, or parts thereof if the profit is of a lesser amount. This would vary from company to company and would be personal.

There must be other rewards during the year. Meals for staff and spouses, local trips, lottery tickets, morning teas, international trips, and so on. The celebrations would not just be for successes but for the odd failures too, as this will generate more risk-taking and greater innovations.

When the whole system supports and directs the company's people towards products and services delivered in a manner and cost that cannot be matched, the competition will be left behind. This only happens when a company team has fun carrying out work, and has a clear objective they have understood and bought into. The team works best if the reward at the end is for all team members not just for individuals. Lack of recognition of team effort has always been the disadvantage of merit schemes.

The individual is rewarded for personal development through the salary/pay schemes (see Figure 14.2).

When an individual joins the department or area he or she will normally join at the lowest or lower levels, which in Figure 14.2 would be level (D). This is because there would be few individuals who would have the technical and personal skills to fit in at levels above that. These skills would normally be developed only through being part of the department or area's training programme.

From Figure 14.2 it can be seen that there are incremental steps between levels (D) and (C). The value of these steps should be determined by the company, department or area. It would be effective if the company set the system of determining the value of salary/pay at (D) and (A) and then let the department or area determine the steps between these two.

Figure 14.2 Individual payment — through salary and pay

Levels and Incremental Steps

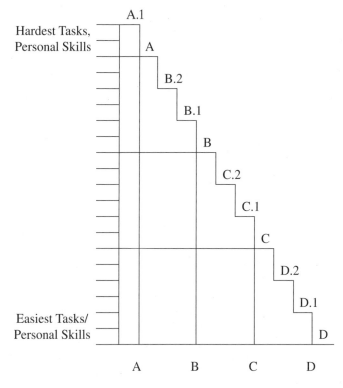

Note: The Technical Skills and Personal Skills matrices work together always; advancement in grade means there has been an improvement in both matrices.

If the person is at level (D) and there are, for example, twenty tasks between (D) and (C), then half that number is ten tasks. If the person becomes suitably skilled in any ten of the tasks, he or she can be paid Level (D.1) and the final ten would achieve salary/pay Level (D.2). The increments are to encourage and give payment, through salary or pay, for the individual to:

- become more skilled
- become more valuable to the company
- become better developed
- have a broader knowledge of the business in that area
- be better able to make better decisions
- be more skilled at directed risk taking.

The increments may be of 15 per cent of the difference between Levels (D) and (C). So if the difference was $2000, each step would be worth $300. The big jump in pay would be when the individual moved from Level (D/D.1/D.2) to (C/C.1/C.2). This would depend on the skill levels achieved by the individual. A suitable move on the Personal Skills Matrix would also be necessary.

In some companies there is a limit to the number of people in each grade of salary. This is to ensure that there is a margin of competition in the system. The limit is within the whole of the level. If it was decided to have thirty Level (C)s, then that would include all (C)s [C/C.1/C.2] thereby allowing all the Level (C)s to achieve Level (C.2) while Level (B) remains unavailable. Other companies have no limits.

As the assessments are carried out every six months, it is possible for some staff to move down the matrix if they have not maintained their technical and personal skill levels. This ability to move up and down ensures that these people continually maintain their skills, keeping up to date with changes to the way the company does business, and the like.

When a slot becomes available the best and most *qualified* person will move to the next level (if there are limits).

Qualified means that the person is already qualified to the next full level, i.e. if at Level (D.2), the person is qualified to Level (C) already, before the slot becomes available.

Best means the person who is the best, *not the longest serving* member, will be selected by the assessment team for the slot.

There is *no annual merit* or incremental scaling of salaries in this system. The *only* way to improve salary or pay is to develop more technical and personal skills.

Summary

The system ensures that everyone receives payment through their salary or pay for personal development, as determined through the matrices, and this is the *individual*'s personal recognition.

The performance rewards are earned by everyone in the company's team if the company does well and that is the driver for the *team*. There is no time for walls, empires or territories now as the reward at the end of the year, for example, is dependent on the whole company doing well. If one department or area does well and everyone else suffers because of the tactics used, then everyone suffers as no one gets anything.

Performance is no longer the responsibility of one individual, but now becomes *the result* of all the company's individuals working together as a team. As the company team learns to work increasingly as an effective and efficient team, so the performance reward will grow and grow as a result. Peers and other company team members will encourage each other to do better and for the customers to be happier and more satisfied with the company's products and services.

A German study showed that men who are kissed by their spouse or lover before they leave for work live five years longer and earn 15 per cent more than those who are not kissed.

So, *the team wins.*

The team will demand, design and implement excellent communications to ensure that the customers are excited by the service and products the company delivers and will come back for more, bringing with them people they know.

The system delivers payments and rewards where it should (individual and team) and cancels the poor aspects of merit and annual increments (given just because twelve months have passed). No longer do the *longest serving* have the right to move through the system; moreover this new system drives company staff to support each other and, especially, the customer at every opportunity.

15

Visiting others

Many companies and departments start the process but revert to the old ways of doing things simply because the apparent confusion does not seem to be worth the end result. This is especially true of those companies and departments that do not have staff with previous experience of involvement in change of this magnitude.

It can be helpful to visit other departments within your company and other companies which have experienced a successful restructuring. Talking to others who have been through a 'team environment' process is worth every minute spent.

It is very important to visit other companies on a regular basis. How many companies have you formally visited in the last twelve months? If the answer is fewer than four, then it is time to adjust your diary. Also, if you are part of the management team, you must encourage your staff to visit companies. Most often the staff will do this without expecting payment beyond reimbursement of petrol money.

The visit should be well structured with your company's team having prepared:

- a list of what the visiting person or team is interested in (this should be sent to the company in advance to enable those receiving you to be well prepared)
- a list of questions you would like answered (this can be sent ahead too, to allow for the preparation of answers to questions which may be difficult to answer on the spot).

If the visit is part of a project of information collection aimed at several companies, then the list of questions (questionnaire) should if possible, remain fixed, so that data received is consistent for evaluation purposes. A copy of the report should then be sent to those companies visited, if commercially possible, to assist in fostering relationships. You can also invite the staff of companies visited to visit your company in return.

Make a plan for, say, six months ahead and get volunteers to set up the visits in accordance with an agreed checklist.

16

Conclusions

Look at your company today. In your wildest dreams you probably could not have designed the bureaucracy, systems, procedures, policies, forms, numbers of approval signatures and crazy steps that exist there today and which prevent effective business from happening.

Of the hundreds of thousands of companies in the world, the few hundred really successful ones have achieved more than success: they have also become the envy of other companies. What have those successful companies done that others have not? What enabled these few to succeed?

Fear is one reason why there are so few genuine and lasting successes today. This includes fear for one's job and security, and applies to both management and non-management. Perhaps, in this new team environment, the team can do without someone, maybe me! To overcome this fear some companies have in place a no-lay-off system. But they were only able to institute this after they had shed the past.

Fear also includes fear of the unknown. Maybe someone will have to justify why a mistake was made in this new directed risk-taking environment. Mistakes are OK in this new environment, but what happens then? If the company's reaction is to 'take the stick' to these mistakes instead of asking what everyone has learnt from them, the change will be doomed.

Management fear that they may be found wanting and not know everything, and that is also unsettling. Fear is the great wall behind which many people (not just management) hide. However, the wall is only in the mind. It was built by previous conditioning and the old environment within the company. All people must work together to change the environment to one in which trust and directed risk-taking are normal.

Fear makes people create visions of all the negative 'what ifs' and these become the inhibitors. If these same people can infect enough people with their fears, the whole process will be effectively stopped.

Companies must drive out fear and achieve an environment in which management get excited by people changing 'the way the company does business'. This will achieve:

- unparalleled service, product quality, and reliability
- response times that are the envy of other companies
- consistency, allowing costs to fall away and margins to grow
- profitable market share and growth previously restricted to monopolies
- a company image and reputation that makes customers talk about the company to the people they know, resulting in long-term loyalty
- company strength to be obtained, nurtured and driven from within, instead of being the result of freak or unusual external circumstances or world occurrences.

This book outlines a system which is simple to use, if you can take the risk. It enables companies, departments and areas to carry out every step of the process to ensure that staff and all their actions are *adding value* to the delivery of products and services to the customers.

A very short list of the value-adding areas discussed in this book is given below.

Topic	**Adds value to the CUSTOMER and:**
Matrix	The whole person **(value/quality)** • career development • technical skills • personal skills • knowledge • department/area control

	• customer sensitivity • business objectives achievement
Eliminate/shorten processes	The way the company does business Constant improvements
Assessments	Improve: • quality • reliability • consistency • training (direct investments) • people development • what and when to train
JPGs	Self learning Training Innovation Evaluating work content Business processes/customer service
Quality Structure	Processes Products/services Common: • language • techniques • skills Communications
Project Teams	All aspects of the business Staff skills, knowledge & development Constant improvements
Business Plan	Mission accomplishment: • company • department • people

Functions	Business plan and company
Tasks	Functions and company
Training	Time spent in training Staff development Job skill improvement Quality and consistency Decision making Service/products
Trust	People, environment and company
Proof of the need	Everything by everyone
Structure	Communication Empowerment Enabling
Company environment	Company Teams/people
Culture	Total team effort Business results
Salary/pay	Individual and company
Rewards	Teams and company
Agreed objectives	Team effort Results Service/product quality Service/product delivery
Reduction in job titles	Team work/effort Focus on customers Team environment

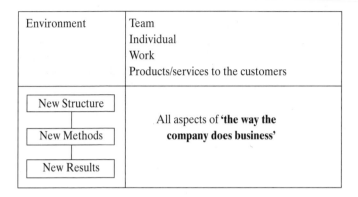

Environment	Team Individual Work Products/services to the customers
New Structure │ New Methods │ New Results	All aspects of **'the way the company does business'**

It is also possible for all the above to have exactly the opposite effect. They must be managed by in-touch and inspired leaders. If the Matrix Concept is established in a company with inspired, in-touch leadership, the company members, suppliers and customers can create the new environment of trust and directed risk-taking. If the company has really achieved a new structure and new methods, then excellent results will follow:

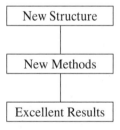

New Structure
│
New Methods
│
Excellent Results

The natural progression of the techniques discussed includes:

- increased spending on training staff, especially the front-line workforce
- responsive business units being created or aligned to only those functions which logically fit together, rather than creating 'total businesses'

- reduction of front-line supervisors and managers
- reduction of corporate management
- having a head office staff not exceeding twenty, and a maximum of ten if the company does less than $500 million per annum in business turnover.

17

Recommendations

In the summary of Chapter 2 the aim of this book was stated as follows:

We want to create a company and environment which:
- is *trusting, rewarding and enjoyable*
- enables the right things to be done, right, first time
- enables staff to be sensitive and responsive to the customer
- enables the implementation of constant improvements to business practices
- creates empowered staff at all levels
- develops good internal and external communications
- recognizes individual as well as team effort and results
- achieves the best possible return on investment
- does not use promotion as the main method of salary reward
- rewards technical and personal skills
- supports teams of staff working to corporate goals
- makes all of the above habitual behaviour.

The two most important aspects of successful companies are:

- developing people
- all aspects of 'the way the company does business'.

The chief ability developed throughout this system is the capability to add value in all the processes discussed. The majority of initial improvements in changing 'the way the company does business' are achieved through no-cost or low-cost changes.

The company must now work out a plan of action which will

enable these changes to be implemented. The plan should be scheduled to commence in the very near future.

The company must provide the capability for:

The new structure will demand new methods, and the new methods will empower and enable the people to achieve the new results.

One final point: It is hard work, but if you are not having fun most of the time at work you might not be doing it right. Doing it right will come only from constant practice, effort and a focus on serving the customer and providing quality products and services.

Two presidents of separate companies were having an argument over which company was 'servicing' the customer better. A third president was there and said, 'I come from a farming background and we take our cows to be *serviced* by the local bull. My company is growing well in the market because we *serve* the customers, and I think the customers have been serviced long enough by your companies.'

Successful business is all common sense, but common sense is clearly not common practice.

Once the Matrix Concept and system is in place it will be difficult to stop, and why would any company want to stop it?

Summary

As seen from the experience of our team, the management decisions of the past have placed the wrong number of people with the wrong skills in the wrong places with great regularity.

In implementing this concept there will be many changes. Whole departments may go and others may be formed through directed efforts. These changes will ensure there will always be changes to 'the way the company does business', directed towards clearly understood company goals.

The staff reductions in the case discussed could well have been staff increases. The process puts emphasis first on doing the right tasks, right, first time, and it then uses these results to determine the right number of people needed and the skills they will require.

The Matrix Concept places emphasis on the whole person.

The system requires top management to be in touch, visionary and inspired. Management are the ones who have made the decisions in the past and they must make the new decisions for today and the future.

The Matrix Concept

Achieving company strength through the development of the total person in each employee, directed at clearly defined and understood goals.

Technical Skills

Personal Skills

Technical Skills Matrix

Personal Skills Matrix

Survey of participating managers

This survey was conducted to determine the impressions of only those middle and senior managers who have actually been through the complete change process as described in this book. The objective was to obtain an unbiased view of the process.

Hence questionnaires were sent to these managers. They were able to hand them in at anytime without their names, positions or companies being known or used. I then had further discussions with them, and without knowing who had written what, was able to draw out more information.

The managers were aged between thirty-three and fifty-two years of age, had all been completely through the change process for a period of more than one year, and had between ten and thirty years' experience in business. Their backgrounds were varied and included police work, the military, a passage straight from school into the company, graduation in commerce and many other experiences. A few of the managers had worked overseas as well as in New Zealand.

The results achieved by the teams in these managers' areas were as described in the following survey.

The survey

The format which follows is: first, the question is posed; second, the answers received are listed under the common areas, with individuals' answers put one after the other, separated by commas; third, a comment is made, reflecting verbal discussions which took place with the managers.

Q. 1 *How would you describe the difference between the previous business structure and the post-matrices structure?*

Previous: fragmented, competition between people and areas, strong demarcation, closed shop and dead-man's shoes.

Post-matrices: cohesive, greater career opportunities, focused training, greater personal development, flat structure, unified teams, 180-degree turnaround from previous, multi-skilling normal and extensive, opportunities for people development and progress, focused on business and customer — not in-fighting.

Comment: 100 per cent stated that, while it was challenging, the process was an excellent learning experience. (Chapter 1.)

Q. 2   *How did you find the initial three weeks of working through the concepts to determine the new structures, single job title, matrices and multi-skilling?*

Mind blowing, exciting, challenging, with trepidation, difficult but very practical, invaluable for moving forward, at last we have business techniques that have been lacking for so long.

Comment: 100 per cent stated that challenging most business views they had held prior to these three weeks was invaluable for changing these same viewpoints. (Chapter 4 onwards.)

Q. 3   *What did you personally find (a) the hardest part of the process of change, (b) the most enjoyable?*

(a) Frustrated at the time so needed to achieve clarity, confronting and motivating people who did not want to change, challenged my attitudes and traditional roles of management, telling some staff they were redundant or at least must move out [of the department].

(b) Watching and furthering successes, openness, achieving business clarity, realizing the 'change' will work this time as it is a system, actually seeing the changes working, seeing people develop.

Comment: 100 per cent stated that the short-term 'pain' was more than worth the long-term gains achieved through this business system. (Chapter 13.)

Q. 4   *What was your view of the change achieved, after the initial introduction of the concept?*

We achieved in three weeks what we had not achieved in the previous ten years, practical and logical approach, great potential, this time it will work, not sure it would work, was initially sceptical to say the least but gratified by the results.

Comment: 87 per cent stated they still feared after the first period of two months that it could fail, but by that time they wanted success as it was a complete system, and felt it was achievable. Fifteen per cent felt it would succeed after the initial three weeks. (Chapter 8.)

Q. 5   *What is your view of the changed department today?*

Totally successful with scope to improve still (a mental attitude where change is normal), practical and logical approach, the only way to go if we want to be successful, it is a success, excellent, best thing that ever happened.

Comment: 100 per cent stated that the management had to have a common and agreed vision for ongoing success, the vision of all areas going through the same matrix process and removing the barriers throughout the organization. (Chapter 14.)

Q. 6   *What problems did you experience in determining functions and tasks? (i.e. What 'should' the department be doing?)*

Once the department mission and business plan were agreed

upon it made it easier, overcoming preconceived ideas, lack of personal expertise in some areas, deciding the difference between what the customer wanted and needed and managing that, lack of documentation on what we were doing at that time, using new ways, inconsistency of the work the department was doing, there were so many redundant functions and tasks it was hard to know where to start.

Comment: 100 per cent agreed upon the need for a strong facilitator and felt it would have taken two months or more (if ever) to determine the mission, business plan, functions and tasks if it were not for the process itself being so complete and logical. (Chapter 5.)

Q. 7 (a)   *What do you feel are the advantages of the Technical Skills and Personal Skills matrices?*

(a)   We needed to combine individuals into teams and the matrices and system achieved this and we all gained support skills, allows people to concentrate on 'units' of a job and progress in a logical manner, induces individuals to advance themselves while still being a full team member, provides incentive to widen skills and attributes and become a valuable employee, relates to people not position, provides clear career path, provides opportunities, it accurately lets people know 'where they are' and what they need to achieve to improve.

Comment: 100 per cent stated this system (or something very like it) is just what was missing from companies they have worked for/with. The ability to update, improve and operate the system at departmental level is just another major advantage of the system.

(b)   *What are the disadvantages of the matrices?*

(b)   What disadvantages are there in being a complete

person?, in large areas too much multi-skilling could affect excellence but managed well gives the correct balance, getting acceptance of other divisions or departments who want to hold on to the 'old ways' of doing business.

Comment: In discussions with these managers, a common concern was heard regarding the company's commitment to training. If times get hard, the training budget should be maintained or increased as results of the system, which include training, clearly demonstrate the positive effects. (Results are discussed in the Introduction and in Chapters 7 and 9.)

Q. 8   *What problems were experienced during the initial selection of the non-management people for the new environment once the matrices and 'single job title' structures were created (during the initial three weeks)?*

Lack of hard data on the individuals to compare them to the new job requirements, many staff had their last personal review six years ago or more, making these value judgements on individuals with limited information, sleepless nights as most staff were known to us but this did make the selection easier, trying to balance teams in technical and personal skills, resistance from longer serving staff, uncertainty among staff during the three weeks of initial work when they did not know the results, unions resisting initially.

Comment: 100 per cent of these managers spoke of the enormous change they had to make personally. To go from the 'state-owned' type of company mentality and fuzzy systems that loved bureaucracy and levels to this one of clarity, control, empowerment, productivity, fun, no empires, etc. placed a large demand on them personally. (Chapter 9.)

Q. 9   *When carrying out assessments of the staff's progress every six months, what are the problems of developing and evolving the assessment method?*

Breaking down the thinking locked in by years of the 'HAY' system, having never done this before as it was a new concept, each assessment period the process improves as we refine it, achieving clarity on what is possible to measure, weighting the important tasks and skills, simply developing a thorough system, flow charting processes would help/helps, need some written tests.

Comment: All these managers endorsed the six-month assessment period as giving all staff a road map of training and development for the following six months. As the assessment results in a personal letter detailing areas that need personal development, the next six months is very focused and value adding to the individual, team, company and customer. As the development relies on peer support, the team is strengthened. All staff are fully involved in improvements to the system. (Chapter 11.)

Q. 10 *How were the staff informed, coached and assisted towards accepting the whole system and assessment process?*

Formal and informal discussions and training, advantages of the new methods were shown (as opposed to the old ways), that the completeness of salaries/matrices/assessments/training could only be achieved through this new system of doing business, everyone went through a trial assessment (fun run) to enable (1) management to get it right and (2) staff to experience and comment on the process.

Comment: 100 per cent agreed the 'fun run' was a vital first step before the real assessments were carried out. Staff and management sat down and discussed what happened and how to improve the system and this takes the mystery and surprises out of the assessment process. (Chapters 4 and 9.)

Q. 11 *How has training affected the development of the change process?*

Training is paramount to achieving change as it has broadened everyone's vision of what was and is possible, it clearly helps and needs to be focused/planned/evaluated, which the system provides, training helped staff (management and non-management) to understand the radical changes, following the TQM/business/personal skills training progress was accelerated and more enjoyable.

Comment: Without exception these managers stressed the value of training and the need for everyone to go through the training designed for the following twelve months. The training gave ease of communication as it also included common business tools, language, reporting format and system, and team membership training. Even those staff who felt they 'knew it anyway' have stated they learned from the training. New techniques and ways of leading, being a team member, providing customer service, and so on require constant, focused training. The ability to focus the training on the department's requirements was also unanimously stated as a major advantage, rather than the 'corporation doing it to you' approach.

This raises the questions of changes which must occur in corporate areas; and of what really enables the company members to be skilled at providing the right products and services, in the right manner, at the right price; and of what constitute organizational dinosaurs?

The training used in this focused training environment and system included making use of actresses and opera singers, sailing, hi-jacking the staff, mixed teams from the whole department, outdoor experiences, etc. Does this sound like the training in your area or company? (Chapter 12.)

Q. 12   *How would you describe your (management's) role in the change process?*

To implement the new system is like attempting to conduct an orchestra with only limited musical knowledge, supportive and enthusiastic, coach/motivator/assessor, encouraging, picking up the concepts and techniques and applying them to the environment within and outside of the department, defining goals.

Comment: All expressed the importance of consistency in management's demonstration and efforts towards the change. The change from a dictatorial style to a coaching and cheerleader style was difficult for most, but all stated the new empowering environment could produce (and had produced) results which were and are breathtakingly good. (Chapter 13.)

Q. 13   *How important to success were rewards and celebrations?*

Essential, very important, it shows people that the system and management are sincere, lack of rewards / celebration can put a hole in the process.

Comment: All were demanding the need for rewards and celebrations. The types used included dinner for all staff and their partners, private boxes at cricket or rugby grounds, trips, restaurant meals, boat trips, letters of praise and appreciation. The ability for all staff to participate in changing 'the way they do business' was also seen as vital. (Chapters 7 and 14.)

Q. 14   *What made this attempt (and success) at change different from other attempts you have been part of or through over the years?*

A consistent philosophy based on good common sense, we've only really talked and played at change in the past but this was well thought out and practical, achieved good commitment to success by everyone concerned in the early and later stages, this was a philosophy everyone could buy into, a well structured and comprehensive process and not the glossy nonsense lacking substance of the past.

Comment: Everyone felt that the completeness of the system and the opportunity for everyone to accept and *actively participate* in the ongoing system were two very important advantages over other attempts at change. In prior attempts over the past decades attempts involved either management doing something on their own or some other group (corporate) doing it to someone else.

This time everyone had an ongoing part to play which never diminished and each player had to continue doing his or her part for the team and process to work. It is difficult to let the team down when you are being encouraged and supported by everyone. (Chapter 2.)

Q. 15 (a) *Would you go back to the previous way of doing business (i.e. prior to this change process)? (b) Why?*

(a) [100 per cent replied with an emphatic no.]

(b) It is now more fun, organized better, opportunities better, better business results, great environment, great to be part of a high performing team.

Comment: The answers above are limited as most said the same things. The managers answered these questions with a great deal of humour, with comments like 'Need you ask?' and 'Surely you jest?'. It was felt that it would be incredible even to think such a thing and to not continue going forward with even more change.

Summary

Although the questionnaire specifically asked questions to make these managers think 'management' and 'non-management', the environment is very much 'we', with people thinking as individuals in a team and being supportive of the whole team.

The change process is one in which the objective is on the mission of the company to capture and keep customers, to make each customer into a long-term customer and make them want to come back willingly and bring people they know with them.

To achieve this the focus of the system and processes is on the people within the company. The company must take care of its members. The members take care of the customer and the customer will take care of the company.

To do this is so simple, but common sense is still not common practice in business today!

We need everyone rowing the same way!

Case study

An example of a team that has adopted the Matrix Concept and the radical changes required to fully bring about the results this system can offer is the Logistics Department of Air New Zealand (not the company as a whole, but just this one department). This department is now a topic in a book called *Doing it better, Doing it right* (1992: Manor House Press, Wellington) by the New Zealand Minister of State Services, the Rt. Hon. W. F. Birch and Ken Douglas, President of the New Zealand Council of Trade Unions.

All the staff in this department had no idea in December 1990 what they were going to get into when I joined them. They provide a clear example of people who took on this change wholeheartedly and willingly, and who within twelve months brought about startling changes and achieved outstanding results.

Where we were

The department was very much in the State Owned Enterprise (SOE) style where staff worked to specialist roles as individuals, the work environment was one of 'my desk, my phone, my job', and teamwork occurred as the exception rather than as normal practice. Individuals focused on personal goals in their own area rather than supporting the bigger company picture of balancing decisions. It was hard to support the bigger company picture as it was never 'seen'.

The change process

In January 1991 the department management met daily for a period of about three weeks to consider what would be the best work environment in which staff and company could aim towards the goal of working smarter. After considerable effort, the following major changes were decided upon and built into the action plan:

The way we were	*New environment achieved*

• Individuals as individuals
• Multiple job titles
• Vague career path
• Multiple unions
• Vague team goals
• Rewards:
  • vague
  • length of service
 	
• Structured to individual
	• Team required
	• Single job titles
	• Detailed career path
	• Single union
	• Focused/agreed goals
	• Rewards
	  • multi-skilling
	  • personal development
	  • performance
	• Structured to team work

These changes were accomplished in stages similar to those described in this book: missions, business plans, functions, tasks, matrices, assessments, project letters, etc. Staff numbers were right-sized to the new environment, where multi-skilling replaced much of the old specialist attitudes.

All remaining staff were given a four-hour presentation on the new environment and structure which they had, in interviews, agreed to become part of. All staff were selected against more than eighty criteria (in the new system) and the most important was '*ability to be an effective team member* '.

Impacts felt during the change

Some staff (both management and non-management) did not believe that the changes would stick. Scars from previous failed attempts at change had not healed and this had to be overcome. The method used was to get all the staff involved in reorganizing the department layout so it would be conducive to teamwork, effective communication, cross-training, etc. This structural change to the department enabled everyone, inside and outside the department, to see the changes and to see that this time the changes were there to stay.

Right-sizing the staff numbers encouraged staff to accept learning new methods of doing business including Total Quality Management, as the smaller numbers could not cope with the old workloads. The two-day TQM training was tailored to a service industry and specifically to airline work, and it focused on 'right things, right, first time'.

Project teams of volunteers were established to rid the area of wasteful practices. The teams were also an excellent training ground for development of the staff's business and presentation skills. The teams worked extremely well; having a single job title had removed the seniors and juniors, and the new team spirit had to be watched and coached by management.

The management changed their title from the Management Team to the Support Team, to remind all management staff what their daily role is: to support the operations staff in doing their jobs better through providing resources, training, coaching, cheerleading, celebrating and so on. This was quite a change from the SOE management style!

Some results

We went through all the problems discussed in this book. Staff had participated voluntarily in the total review and layout of the office and other projects, and within the first ten months of the process the following were some of the measurable results (determined through analysis of the 1991 year):

- 35 per cent reduction in operating costs
- 73 per cent reduction in overtime payments
- 35 per cent reduction in penal rates
- 89 per cent reduction in job titles/levels (nine down to one)

- reduction in unnecessary assets
- 31 per cent increase in staff value (technical and personal skills)
- 38 per cent increase in productivity
- 148 per cent increase in On-Job-Training (in-department)
- 120 per cent increase in external training
- 178 per cent increase in multi-skilling.

All these figures were assessed and proved through measurements and assessments.

The department had accomplished TQM and a team environment exactly as described in all the theory books. However, this is not a theory but a fun, active, challenging environment where there are no sacred cows. Everything is questioned and constant improvements are a normal part of the day's business. This is a total service industry, and the accomplishments were outstanding. The team members are demanding, and getting, more and more changes and improvements, big and small.

Staff are willing to work outside their normal, accepted hours to keep the customer satisfied, without claiming all possible award payments.

Team members, with their peers, designed the office layout to be the best possible, designed shift patterns to be user friendly yet cost effective and workload sensitive, and improved and are still improving communication. Training is focused and critiqued by all to improve future training and expenditure. It is an environment created by the team members in which information is freely given and rumours no longer survive.

Tours

The department even operates tours for other Air New Zealand departments and outside companies. Some of the companies who have had CEOs, Senior GMs, GMs, Senior Managers, Managers and staff on tours include: New Zealand Steel,

Anchor Butter, Mackay Shipping, Group Rentals, BASF Chemicals, Next Electronics, Tasman Express Line.

The department is in two levels: non-management (called the Operations Team) who all have one job title of Logistics Controller and the two matrices, and management who are called the Support Team.

The tours were designed and are run by the Operations Team members and no Support Team members are present during the conference room presentations. This in itself, when you look at the position levels of visitors on the tours, is a clear indication of the trust which exists in the department between the Support Team and the Operations Team. This trust ensures the existence of a very good Logistics Team.

New hires

When staff are being hired into the department the Operations Team has members who participate fully in the interviews. This is an obvious and logical thing to do because the new hires will work with all Logistics staff.

Summary

The above are just some of the radical results and changes achieved through this system — but achieved only with the willing and full commitment and effort of *all* those who work in the Logistics Team. It is a startling example to any who want to see the effects of the process detailed in this book.

To all businesses which are changing to become people companies, I offer my very best wishes for your future.

Further Reading

Bardwick, J. *Danger in the Comfort Zone*. (ANACOM Books).

Beer, R., Eisenstat, R. A., and Spector, B. *The Critical Path to Corporate Renewal*. (Harvard Business School Press).

Belasco, J. *Teaching the Elephant to Dance*. (Crown Publishers).

Bradford, L. and Raines, C. *Twenty Something*. (Mastermedia Ltd.).

Greenburg, E. R. *Customer Service*. (American Management Association).

Hewlett, S. A. 'The Boundaries of Business: The Human Resource Deficit', *The Harvard Business Review* (1991) Jul/Aug.

Kaplan, R., Drath, W., and Kofodimos, J. *Beyond Ambition*. (Jossey-Bassi).

Maurer, R. *Caught in the Middle*. (Productivity Press).

Ott, R. *Creating Demand*. (Business One Irwin).

Peters, T. *In Search of Excellence*. (Random House).

Stayer, R. 'How I let my people lead', *Harvard Business Review* November/December 1990.

The Fellows of Harvard. *Strategy*. (Harvard Business School Press).

Walton, M. *Deming Management at Work*. (G. P. Putnam and Sons).